Robert Irwin's Power Tips for Selling a House for More

Other McGraw-Hill Books by Robert Irwin

Robert Irwin's Power Tips for Selling a House for More

Robert Irwin

McGraw-Hill

New York   San Francisco   Washington, D.C.   Auckland   Bogotá
Caracas   Lisbon   London   Madrid   Mexico City   Milan
Montreal   New Delhi   San Juan   Singapore
Sydney   Tokyo   Toronto

McGraw-Hill

A Division of The McGraw·Hill Companies

1 2 3 4 5 6 7 8 9 0   DOC/DOC   0 9 8 7 6 5 4 3 2 1 0

ISBN 0-07-136277-0

It was set in Baskerville per the BSF TTS design by the Professional Book Group's composition unit, Hightstown, N.J.

Printed and bound by R. R. Donnelley & Sons Company.

McGraw-Hill books are available at special quantity discounts to use as premiums and sales promotions, or for use in corporate training programs. For more information, please write to the Director of Special Sales, Professional Publishing, McGraw-Hill, Two Penn Plaza, New York, NY 10121-2298. Or contact your local bookstore.

This book contains the author's opinions. Some material in this book may be affected by changes in the law (or changes in interpretations of the law) or changes in the market conditions since the manuscript was prepared. Therefore, the accuracy and completness of the information contained in this book and the opinions based on it cannot be guaranteed. Neither the author nor the publisher is engaged in rendering investment, legal, tax, accounting, or other similar professional services. If these services are required, the reader should obtain them from a competent professional.

Contents

Preface

Every house can be sold—the only differences are how long it will take and how much you will get. As a seller, you want a fast sale, for the most money.

Yet, that's not easy to achieve. The rules for selling a house have changed. Today, buyers are far more sophisticated than they were just a few years ago. They are prepared to low-ball a seller, to reopen negotiations after a deal has been struck (based on disclosures and inspections), to even refuse to conclude a sale until they get their way.

Furthur, the rules for dealing with agents are also changing.

Negotiating commissions and obtaining lower cost fee-for-services are becoming increasingly prevalent.

Even the market itself is different—in recent years it's been very hot making it difficult to get a realistic estimate of a house's true market value. As a result, some sellers have received less than they should for their homes. What sellers need is to get ahead of the curve, to get a leg up on buyers. That's what this insider book offers—powerful tools that top investors and agents use to get a home sold fast, and for more.

In it you'll see how to get your price in any market, hot or cold. How to handle buyers who want to "steal" your property, how to negotiate with agents, even how to better dress up your home to showcase its curb appeal. It also explains the importance of controlling the escrow, how to auction your property, and what to do to avoid higher taxes.

My goal in writing this book is to put sellers on an even playing field with buyers. If you're thinking of selling your home, or are already in the sales process, this book will vastly improve your chances of getting a far better deal for you!

Robert Irwin

Robert Irwin's
Power Tips
for Selling a
House for More

1

Move Your Home, Fast

Power Tip 1
Six Ways to Get Multiple
Offers

Your goal is to get the highest price for your home in the shortest time possible. One way to do this is to get buyers to compete to purchase your property. In a competition, buyers are more likely to pay the full asking price. When the market's super hot, they may even offer more than you're asking! The trick becomes how to market your house—how to make it so appealing that buyers simply can't help themselves and feel compelled to make offers.

Can you really do this? Of course, but how successful you'll be depends to a large degree on the housing market in your community at the time. In any market, however, here are six steps that will work to get you a better price, faster:

1. *Price it right.* You want a high price for your property, but if you price it too high, buyers may simply ignore it. They may feel you're an "unmotivated seller" who simply doesn't understand market value and who will be too difficult to deal with. On the other hand, if you price it correctly, right at true market value, it's much more likely to get noticed. And being noticed is the first critical step toward getting your price.

> It's better to have five buyers checking your property out at a fair price than no buyers checking it out at a price that is too high.

Remember, the goal is to get lots of buyers excited about your house. The more there are, the more likely you are to receive better offers. Agents quickly let their buyers know when a property is hot and buyers then feel motivated to act, giving you their best offer.

Beware, however, of carrying this too far. To generate even more interest, some tricky sellers price their houses slightly below market. Their hope is to set off a buying frenzy where would-be buyers compete and force the price up ever higher. The danger here, of course, is that you might get only one offer at your below-market asking price, and even if you didn't accept it, you probably would owe a commission to the agent!

Depending on how the listing is written, agents are usually entitled to a commission when they bring in a buyer who's "ready, willing, and able" to purchase, not when the sale is actually completed. If you price it low and get a full-price offer, you might have to pay a commission, even if you decide not to sell.

2. *Dress it for sale.* If you went into a clothing store and saw a pair of slacks you liked but upon closer inspection saw a stain on them, would you buy them? If you're like most people, you'd put them back and look elsewhere. Or, if you were particularly good at haggling, you might offer to take them off the store's hands at half the price, hoping to get the stain out yourself.

Selling you house is similar. If there are any defects (peeling or faded paint, cracks in walls or floors, stains on carpeting, and so on), buyers will shy away. The only ones who will make you an offer are those who treat the property as a fixer-upper ("handyman special"), and you can be sure they'll make low-ball offers that you won't find appealing.

Therefore, *before* offering your house for sale, fix it up. Get it to look as it did when it was new—even better! The more work you do at this stage, the better your chances for a quicker sale at a higher price. (See also Chapter 5.)

3. *Market the sizzle.* You may believe that if you have a better mousetrap, people will beat a path to your door to buy it. But you'd be wrong about that. At any given time, there are over a million and a quarter houses for resale in the country. That's a lot of property.

It's up to you to let buyers know that the house you have is on the market. You will wait a very long time for them to search you out on their own. To that end, you need to market it. That means the following:

- List your house with a hot agent, and be sure your listing is placed both on the MLS and on the Internet.

- See that the house is promoted everywhere, even if you must pay for some advertising. That includes the local papers, "Houses for Sale" web sites, local TV public access stations, transfer offices of corporations—you name it. It also means having a large, visible "For Sale" sign on the property.

- Be sure other agents know about it. That means seeing to it your agent "caravans" the property (shows it around) and "talks it up" at agent meetings.
- Tell everyone you know, including agents, friends, family associates, lovers—everyone.

Don't knock word-of-mouth to find a buyer. I once sold a house to a person with whom I struck up a conversation on a commuter airplane flight!

4. *Be a tough negotiator.* If you want a high price, convince buyers that it's in their interest to give it to you. Too many sellers are passive when it comes time to negotiate an offer. They leave it up to their agent, their attorney, or to no one at all. As a result, either they look weak to a buyer (meaning they eternally get low offers) or unmotivated (meaning buyers simply stop negotiating).

Present buyers with a prepared list of comparable sales to justify the price you are asking. Point out the number of lookers and prospective buyers who are coming by, indicating that other offers are in the works (hopefully they are!). Show off any improvements you've made. Wax poetic about the wonderful neighborhood and high-test scores achieved at the local schools (if there are any). Make the buyers want to pay more for your property and to move onto it quickly.

5. *Convince everyone your house is HOT!* Your first words to a would-be buyer, agent, or anyone else who might be involved in the sale should be, "You know, of course, that this is a hot property and will sell fast for top dollar."

Expect a "ho-hum" response. Agents will be saying to themselves, "Sure, another foolish seller who doesn't know what his or her house is really worth." Prospective buyers may be thinking the same thing.

Then follow up with a killer statistic. "This same house down the street sold last week for $7000 more than I'm asking." (Of course, maybe it was a better located lot or had buyers who didn't know the market and offered too much or whatever.) Or, "There are $15,000 worth of improvements in the house that aren't even calculated into the price." Or, "This was the original model house for the tract and has $30,000 of extra amenities." Or, "I've already turned down a cash offer for $5000 less than I'm asking." Or, you get the idea. Sell the house.

> The old advertising adage that, "It's the sizzle, not the steak that sells," applies to houses, too. If agents and buyers perceive that a house (even one that's higher priced) is hot, it's hot. On the other hand, if they perceive that it's a dog (even if it's lower priced), it's not going to sell as fast or for as much.

6. Try auctioning it off. It's a novel approach that can work well in any market. Check into Tip 51 for details.

Power Tip 2
Become Price Savvy

What is your house worth on the open market? How do you determine its marketable value? Is it worth the amount you owe plus your equity? Is it worth what you paid for it plus 5 percent appreciation per year over the time you've owned it? Is it worth your original cost plus the cost of all the improvements (renovated kitchen, new carpeting, and so on) that you've put in?

The answer is none of these.

Your house is worth only as much as a buyer is ready, willing, and able to pay for it—not a dime more!

The single biggest mistake that sellers make is to overprice their homes. Put your house on the market at a price that is higher than its true value and not only will it sell more slowly, but it may never sell! You may get a lot of lookers who come through scratching their heads trying to figure out why in the world your price is so high. But serious buyers will tend to ignore your house.

This tip is a reality check. It's time for some "Dutch-uncle" talk. If you think I'm being unduly harsh, please grin and bear it. Learning the lessons presented here will save you time and get you a good price.

Three Reasons Sellers Overprice
Their Houses

Do you recognize yourself here?

1. *I've heard prices have gone up.* They have, in most areas of the country. The question is, how much have they gone up in your area? While you may stand to make a profit on a sale, your house may not be the bonanza you think it is. Talk of huge price appreciation in the area of 15 percent a year or more, which has occurred for short bursts in a few parts of the country, may make you see dollar signs. But if the true appreciation is only 3 percent in your area, relying on these inflated figures means you'll price your house right out of the market.

> Don't pay attention to rumors and party gossip about price increases—check them out for accuracy before you set the price for your house.

2. *I've improved my house and I want to get my money back.* Forget it! How much you've put into your house is irrelevant. It doesn't matter if you've spent $50,000 on your kitchen and $25,000 in landscaping. If the market says your house is only worth $10,000 more because of these improvements, that's all you'll get. The second biggest mistake that sellers make is to think that buyers (or anyone else for that matter) care one whit about how much sweat, tears, and money they've poured into the house. The harsh and sometimes hard to hear truth is that no one but you cares.

> Listen carefully. As hard as it may be to hear, improvements don't always return dollar for dollar spent. This is why you must be very judicious when you decide what to improve. Check out my *Tips & Traps When Renovating Your Home* for a detailed explanation on how to determine which improvements return the most when it's time to sell.

3. *I want a certain profit after I pay off my loan and the real estate commission.* Everybody is in this boat. Unfortunately, it's got a leaky bottom. Do you seriously think that any buyer cares how much you owe or how much it's going to cost you in commission (and other closing costs) to sell your house? Buyers only care how much it's going to cost them in down payment (cash) and mortgage (monthly payments). They're looking to get into your property for the lowest possible cost, not to give you the highest profit.

Forget about what you owe and what you want out of your house. You can only get what the market will bear, not a dime more.

How Can I Know What the Market Value of My House Really Is?

Any agent worth his or her salt can provide you with a comparative market analysis (CMA). This will show you what houses comparable to yours have sold for in your area. Since buyers look to previous sales prices to establish value, this is where your house's price should be.

If there have been four comparable sales in the last 6 months with the highest at $225,000 and the lowest at $210,000, all else being equal, what do you think the price range for your house is? If you answered $250,000 because of the new bathroom you put in, that's not right.

If you answered $240,000 because prices have gone up, again that's incorrect.

If you answered $235,000 because that's how much you need to cover the cost of paying off your mortgage, commission, and closing costs, again you're wrong.

> Remember, your house is only worth what the market will bear as determined by recent sales of comparable houses.

Buyers today are sophisticated and they will insist on a CMA before they make an offer. They'll be looking at the same figures as you are. If you're too high, they'll make an offer on someone else's house.

Other Sources for a CMA

In addition to agents, you can also get a look at comparables by checking various web sites. I've found the following to be helpful (note some charge for the service):

www.homeadvisor.com

www.dataquick.com

www.monsterdata.com

Become a Buyer for a Weekend

The best course of action, however, that I can suggest is that for at least one weekend you take off your seller's hat and become a buyer. You can do it yourself by going around to "Open Houses" or more easily by having an agent prepare a tour for you of comparable houses currently for sale and recently sold (which are usually just pass-bys). Simply and honestly tell the agent you're interested in selling your house and may want to list with him or her. But, you want to see what's on the market first. Any good agent will be happy to give you a tour in the hope of landing you as a listing.

There's no better awakening to what the market is truly like than getting out there and looking at your competition. You may find that there are dozens of similar houses offered for sale at far less than you imagined yours was worth. Or, you could be shocked to discover that there are few houses on the market and those similar to yours are going for far more than you anticipated, meaning you can ask a higher price!

The big advantage of being a buyer-for-a-weekend is that you're not taking anyone else's word for it. You're seeing for yourself, and there's nothing in the world more convincing.

Power Tip 3
Build an Action Plan

Think of selling your house as a journey. You want to get from here
to there, and you need an itinerary to help you do it. You want to get
from ownership to sale, and a plan of action will help you to accomplish that goal.

The advantage an action plan offers is that it breaks things down
into smaller, simpler steps. While overall the sale of your house may
seem intimidating, even impossibly difficult, break it down into its
parts and it become doable, even easy!

In order to create an action plan that will result in selling your
house for more, you need to first answer three basic questions.
Don't contact an agent, paint a room, or put up a sign until you've
addressed these three questions.

Three Questions to Ask

1. *How fast must you sell?* Some sellers can take all year. They
don't need to move. They're content to stay in their houses until
they get their price. They're in no hurry. They can afford to wait
until they get their price.

Other sellers must move quickly. It could be a job transfer, a
divorce, a death or illness in the family, or anything else that puts the
pressure on. You must get rid of that house, fast. You can't afford to
wait for a high price. You've got to get out, now.

What's interesting is that often the person who must move
quickly ends up not only with a faster sale than the person who
can afford to wait but also with a higher price! Sometimes the
excitement generated in buyers by a highly motivated seller
produces higher offers.

---

2. *What is roughly your bottom price?* It could be any amount or
none at all. Perhaps below a certain price you'd rather stay in the
house than move. It certainly would be to your advantage to think
this through up front. Once you decide, then determining an asking

price and negotiating down (if necessary) becomes much easier.

On the other hand, perhaps you don't have a bottom price. You just have to get out. Knowing this up front is also helpful. It, likewise, can help you decide on the asking price and with negotiations.

> The danger of setting a bottom price is that it's always arbitrary. In the heat of battle (negotiations) you should always be open to any offer. And always try to turn even the worst offer to your advantage. Being locked into an inflexible bottom price can defeat you here, even before you get started. Better to think of your bottom price as an estimate, rather than as fixed.

3. *What kind of a market are you in?* You need to ask yourself what kind of market conditions are you selling into? In real estate there are three kinds of markets: hot, normal, and cold. A hot market, such as we've had in recent years, means that there are more buyers chasing fewer houses. As a result, houses will often sell as soon as they are listed. It's common to have multiple offers on each house from buyers competing to purchase. And sometimes the houses will even sell for more than their asking price. In this market housing prices are accelerating upward, and your task will be to price your house high enough to take advantage of the lift the market is giving you, without pushing too much and pricing yourself out.

A more normal market finds a fairly large inventory of houses for sale. In the industry this is measured by how long it takes to sell the average house. A sale time of 60 to 120 days is usually considered normal. In this type of market you'll need to promote your house far more in order to get offers. And you can expect those offers to almost always start out below your asking price. Your challenge here is to convert low-ball offers to higher ones that you can accept.

A truly cold market doesn't happen often in real estate, but it did exist from the end of the 1980s into the middle 1990s. Houses were listed for a year or more without any offers. Prices were falling, in some areas as much as 30 to 40 percent off their previous highs. There was a huge inventory of unsold houses and almost no buyers.

In this type of market, you must literally stand on your head to get a sale. This can mean trying auctions, offering incentives (such as low-interest-rate loans, TV sets to agents who produce buyers, larger commissions, and so forth.) It takes much harder work, but you can get offers. Your challenge is to accept less than you hoped for and get out before the price goes even lower!

Once you've identified the market and discovered how highly (or lowly) motivated your are, as well as what your bottom line may be, you're ready to proceed with your action plan for selling your house.

Plan Your Action

Here's a typical battle plan for selling a house. It mirrors the following chapters in this book:

1. *Find an agent.* Most sellers will use an agent. You want one that's loyal, obedient, assertive (with buyers), honest to a fault, and ever attentive.

2. *Save on the commission.* In today's market discount brokers are popping up everywhere, especially on the Internet. If you're willing to assume some of the burden of the sale, you can save a bundle.

3. *Sell it yourself.* Never mind using an agent—do all the work and save all the commission. About 10 percent of all house sellers take this approach.

4. *Dress up the property.* Before showing the house to any buyer, get it in shape. Think of it as going to a grand ball. You wouldn't show up in dirty coveralls. You'd come in a gown or tux. Dress your house accordingly.

5. *Demand a big deposit.* It helps lock in the buyer and ensures that the deal will go through.

6. *Negotiate a higher price.* Don't be prepared to accept a buyer's first (or second) offer. Learn how to counter in order to get more from every offer.

7. *Be honest on disclosures.* Don't lie or diminish defects in the property. Your house is what it is. Let the buyers know and protect yourself in the process.

8. *Insist the buyers get a professional inspection.* This protects you, too! Later on, it makes it more difficult for the buyers to say they didn't know about a defect that suddenly appears.

9. *Control the escrow.* Manage the deal after you get an offer to be sure it closes on time with no problems.

10. *Save on your closing costs.* Act early and negotiate the fees to save yourself big bucks.

Sell Fast, and for More

Your plan of action will enable you to shoot past other sellers who are stumbling along. You'll operate at high speed throughout the entire transaction.

2

How to Find a Hot Agent

Power Tip 4
Find an Agent Who's
Plugged In

The most important attribute of an agent when it comes to finding buyers for your house is that he or she be fully connected to the real estate system. The more active and involved with other agents he or she is, the greater the chance your agent will produce a suitable buyer quickly.

To understand why this works, it's helpful to see things from the perspective of a not-so-wonderful agent. For too many agents, the business is more a matter of survival than of outstanding achievement. This means soliciting as many listings as possible, putting them on the Multiple Listing Service (MLS), and then waiting for other agents to discover and sell them. This type of agent is known in the trade as a *lister*. Indeed, there's even an old adage that goes, "Those who list, last," suggesting that the way to survive is to get as many listings signed up as possible.

This may be okay for the agent, but it's not okay for you. You want an agent who does more than simply sign you up and move on. You want an agent who actively works to sell your property.

Talking Up the Listing

Many sellers are surprised when they learn that the biggest single plus that an agent can bring to a listing is the determination and ability to spread the word among other agents. It all has to do with exposure.

In real estate, the more exposure your property has, the greater the chance that the right potential buyer will hear about it—and make an offer. And the greatest avenue of getting exposure is through other agents.

> It's a mistake to think that you'll get greater exposure for your house through newspaper advertising, public open houses, or even Internet listings. The greatest exposure comes from a good agent spreading the word about your property to other agents.

Notwithstanding the inroads that the Internet and For Sale by Owners (FSBOs) have made, it remains a fact that more than 80 percent of all buyers today are still led to the property they purchase by flesh and blood agents. The agents scout out the properties, and then show them to their clients—your buyer.

The difficulty is that in any given area there are often thousands of properties listed. As a result, it's difficult for even the best agents to be aware of all or even a large portion of the properties. That's where your listing agent comes in. A good listing agent will make sure that every other agent in the area hears about your property. This can take many forms.

- The best way to spread the word is by direct contact. Your agent stands up at a meeting of local agents (typically held weekly or at least monthly) and tells everyone in attendance about this spectacular house (yours) he or she has for sale, why it will sell quickly and why other agents should jump on it.

- Your agent sends faxes, e-mails, and makes phone calls to other agents spreading the word about your property.

- Caravaning is another method: your agent holds an open house for agents only (not the general public). Most realty companies now caravan (tour recent listings) on a regular basis. But a good agent will not only just keep the house open, but will provide food and drink (typically sandwiches, desert, and coffee) in addition to induce other agents to come by and take a look. This is a major selling tool that should not be overlooked.

- Your agent gets you to offer a bonus to the selling agent. When your listing agent says to you, "Why not offer the selling agent an extra $1/2$ percent commission, or a free TV set, or a free short vacation, or some other bonus," don't think he or she is trying to do you a disservice by jacking up the commission. Actually, the agent is asking you for help in exposing your property. If your lister can stand up at an agents' meeting and say, "Not only is this property a terrific buy, but my seller will pay the buyer's agent an extra $1/2$ percent commission," all ears will be listening. You won't believe the extra exposure this offers.

A good agent never stops "talking up" your property to other agents and in the process gets your house the exposure it needs to make a sale.

You don't want to reinvent the wheel. There's already a system in place for reaching the greatest number of buyers and that's through the agent network. Use it to your advantage by hiring the agent who's most plugged into it.

How Do You Recognize a Plugged-In Agent?

The moment word hits the street that you're interested in listing your property, you'll be bombarded by agents asking for your listing. Most will be congenial, helpful, sometimes even obsequious. But don't be swayed strictly by personality. (We'll talk about this in the next tip.) Instead, ask point blank, "If I list with you, what will you do to sell my property?"

Expect answers such as, "I'll put a sign in front." Or, "I'll list it on the MLS and on the Internet." Or, "I'll hold an open house for buyers."

It's interesting to note that studies repeatedly have shown that "Open Houses" held for the public (not for agents) rarely produce a buyer for the house that's held open. Rather, Open Houses are seen in the business as a means of getting clients (buyers and sellers) for other properties. In other words, when an agent holds an Open House for the public, chances are he or she is doing more of a favor for himself or herself than for you!

Fine, well, and good. But virtually every agent will do that. You want an agent who gives you additional, better answers:

- I'll talk-up your house at agent meetings, and I attend every one.
- I'll hold special agent-only open houses for your property and spend my own money on snacks to get better attendance.
- I'll offer bonuses (if you'll cooperate) to the buyer's agent.
- I'll spend every available hour of my time letting other agents know your house is for sale and what a terrific deal it really is.

When an agent tells you this, you've got one who understands the real nature of the business and is actively involved in the system. Your next step is to ask for at least four references—previously successful sellers who have used this agent. Call them—see if the agent really performed as advertised. If you get resoundingly favorable testimonials, chances are you've got a winner.

Always look for a local agent. An agent can only truly service clients within a relatively small radius, typically 10 to 20 miles. Indeed, it is considered unethical for agents to list property outside of their immediate area, because they cannot properly service their client.

Power Tip 5
Be Comfortable with Your Agent

It's not necessary that you like your agent, but it helps. It's more important, however, that you feel comfortable with him or her in much the same way as you would with any trusted financial advisor.

It's important to understand that your agent is not always going to bring you good news. Yes, you hope that your agent will bring you a deal for full price, cash. However, sometimes you won't like the deal that your agent brings you, or what your agent tells you about the condition of your property, the price, or the terms you're offering. What's important is that you feel the agent isn't pressuring you into something you don't want to do, and that everything that's presented is the agent's honest effort to do the best by you.

Honesty First

Trust in any relationship, financial or otherwise, is built on honesty. You can't trust someone who lies to you, even once. You never know if and when they'll lie again.

Do agent's lie? As a general rule, no. But sometimes a few agents may stretch the truth so that you can hear what you want to hear. For example, you may feel your house is worth $150,000. But the agent tells you that her CMA suggests the true value is closer to $130,000. You scowl and the agent quickly adds, "But there's always a chance we can get it to sell for $150,000."

The agent here is stretching the truth to get the listing. If it's worth $130,000, it's not worth $150,000. That's just plain fact. (See the next tip to understand why.) Nevertheless, no one can say for sure what price any property will bring, so the agent isn't exactly lying, just stretching the possibilities a bit.

Would I list with this agent? Never. I want an agent to tell me the truth up front, the whole truth and nothing but the truth, no matter how distasteful I may find it. I want an agent who says, "I understand why you want $150,000, but I'm sorry to say that's unrealistic. It will sell for $130,000. I'll list it at the lower price. If you want to list it for more, you'd be better off finding another agent."

Will agents really be that honest? The good ones will.

Avoid Pushy Agents

I'm sure you've met this personality type. They fully believe that they know best, not only for themselves but also for you. They pretend to listen to what you're saying, your feelings, your reasoning, and your objections. Then they move right on and tell you what you must do, regardless. If an agent acts this way, he or she is being pushy, and that's something you don't need or want.

Most agents are not pushy, they simply wouldn't last long in the business. But there are degrees to everything. And what I might consider helpfully assertive, you might consider pushy. Therefore, you need to find an agent who fits into your comfort level when it comes to giving advice.

> A good agent will always advise, never demand or insist. The agent will realize it's your house, your money, and your decision and respect that.

It's important that when you're hiring an agent, you spend some time chatting. You can talk about the weather, politics, education, real estate, anything you want. The subject doesn't really matter. What you want to learn is how respectful the agent is of your perspective. An honest agent will occasionally disagree. But a respectful agent will never disparage your opinions or push you to change them by force of will. (A respectful agent might, however, legitimately give you arguments as to why you could be wrong, and then let you decide.)

When first talking with a new agent, I like to let this opening discussion become protracted. The reason is that sometimes pushy people know how they come across and will make an effort to disguise this fact. However, if you talk with them long enough, eventually their true colors come out. If I get a suspicious feeling, I'll arrange for a second or even a third conversation. I would not sign with an agent with whom I did not feel completely comfortable.

Watch Out for the Obsequious Agent

This is the other side of the fence. Here, the agents simply agree with anything you say. Their personality is subservient. You're top dog, and they'll lay down and die if you want. And it's not just to get the listing. They truly worship their clients and would never say anything to give them discomfort.

Not good. Sometimes, as noted, you want your agent to tell you uncomfortable things. This can help you sell quicker for a higher price.

It can be hard to turn down a fawning agent. After all, it's extremely complimentary to have someone hanging on your every word. Nevertheless, remember you want a sale, not a servant.

> You want results, not petting.

Look for the Balanced Approach

It's important to understand that, at some point in the sales process, your agent will be helping you deal with the buyer and the buyer's agent. At that point, you want your agent to be assertive enough to get you a good deal. You want your agent to be pushy enough to get the buyer's agent (and the buyer) to back down.

Remember, rarely (except in very hot markets) will you get a full-price offer for cash. Instead, most buyers will begin by low-balling you. You want your agent to stand up to this and insist on a higher price for you. The last thing you want is, after the buyer's agent has presented the offer, for your agent to look at you with a pathetic smile and say something such as, "Maybe this is the best we can hope for."

You want a positive, assertive response. "My client understands your offer, but our initial reaction is that it's far too low, perhaps even insulting."

No, that's not what they'll say every time, but it's often a good way to begin your end of the negotiations. After all, it does put the buyer's side on the defensive. Now they have to scramble around explaining why the offer's not insulting!

Ultimately, you want an agent with whom you feel comfortable, yet who will have the personality and ability to get the job done for you.

The best agent is one who is a pussycat around you, but a tiger when dealing with the buyers.

Power Tip 6
Let the Agent Help You Set
the Price and Terms

This doesn't mean let the agent set the price. It means allow the agent to give you important input, and then make the price decision yourself.

Make Sure the Agent Gives You a
CMA

As noted in Tip 2, a CMA lets you see what comparable houses are selling for. The agent should prepare this for you without your asking. In fact, the agent should insist that you look at it. Agents who belong to an MLS can usually output this in a few minutes using computer software.

Be sure the CMA includes the following:

- All houses in your price range and area sold within the last 6 months, giving both asking price and eventual sale price. In addition to price, this helps you to establish how much of a discount sellers are giving buyers in order to sell their houses.

- The current inventory. This tells you how many houses are for sale in the area. When you compare it to the average number sold per month, you will have the average time to sell. Typically, it varies between 45 and 180 days. The longer the time to sell, the worse the market. The shorter, the hotter the market.

- The features of the houses that are sold. In order to get a true comparison, you need to know the square footage, the number of bedrooms and baths, whether the property had a choice location or a swimming pool, and so on. (All of this information should be readily available from old listings.) This helps you to determine how similar to yours the sold house was.

The agent should go over each of the houses considering all of these issues and give you direction in how that affects the price you can hope to get for your property.

Listen carefully. A good agent can make a strong case for the proper price, even though it may not be what you want to hear. Or, it could turn out to be more than you anticipated!

Get the Agent's Feel for the Market

A good agent is out there all the time and should be able to tell how the market is performing in the same manner that a soldier can tell you how a battle is going. You can get the information from the front lines.
Agents can often fill you in on:

1. *Whether houses are selling quickly or slowly.* Yes, you can get this information from statistics as noted earlier. But an agent's feeling for what's happening is often more up-to-date and certainly more emotionally involved.

2. *What types of houses are selling?* A few years ago everyone wanted a big two-story house. However, with baby boomers aging, many of them are now looking for single-story houses. Indeed, in many areas of the country the single-story house is commanding a higher price than bigger two-story properties! In some areas condos or co-ops are in demand. An agent can tell you if this applies in your area, and how it will affect the sale of your property.

Buyers also follow trends. Sometimes ranch-style houses are in vogue. Other times, it's southern plantation style. Yet other times, it may be a cottage look. A good agent can fill you in on this and help you price your house up or down, accordingly.

3. *The agent can also help you to understand what kinds of buyers are around in your area.* Are they people working for large corporations transferring in from other parts of the country (who may have big bucks to spend)? Are they mostly first-time buyers trying to squeak by with little cash and difficulty qualifying for financing? Are they mostly families moving up from existing houses

(meaning they must sell their old house in order to buy yours)?
Each type of buyer offers different opportunities and challenges.
A good agent can help you to structure the type of financing you
are willing to accept (perhaps you'll take back a second mortgage
to help a strapped buyer get in), which, in turn, can mean a
quicker sale for a higher price.

An Agent Can Help You with Your Finances

A good agent can help you get a quicker, better financial deal.
Perhaps your house needs lots of cosmetic work to help get it into
shape, but you're strapped for cash. The agent may suggest getting
a short-term home equity loan to help you clean up your property.

Or perhaps you're retiring. You own your house free and clear (or
only have a small mortgage on it). You want income more than cash.
The agent may suggest you carry the first mortgage and, as a result,
get a far higher interest rate than you would otherwise get from the
bank. The agent may help arrange the financing for you.

> Carrying a first mortgage is usually considered a relatively safe
> move, and it can help buyers qualify for your property.

Be Wary If Your Agent Wants You to Set a Low-Ball Price

Sometimes if the market is hot, the agent will ask you to set an arti-
ficially low price to stimulate offers. The idea is to create a sort of
feeding frenzy among buyers who will then bid the price up beyond
your expectations. Beware of doing this. It could backfire if buyers
don't respond. Then you'd be faced with selling at too low a price,
or at the least paying a commission.

Rely on Your Agent

Of course, as with any financial advisor, you should take everything
said with a grain of salt. However, a good agent can help enormously
in pricing your property correctly and getting the best terms for you.

Power Tip 7
Choose Carefully between an
Independent Agent and a
Franchise

I've always advocated choosing the agent over the agency. In other words, pick the right person, regardless of what company he or she works for. This still remains mostly true, although there now are exceptions.

Most significantly, there are relatively few independent agents and companies left in real estate. Almost all agents now work for the giants: Coldwell-Banker, Century 21, Prudential, R/E Max, and other names which have become household words. It's hard for an independent to survive in today's highly competitive atmosphere.

Yet, there are still independent agents and realties out there. They are able to compete because most properties, independent and franchise alike, are still listed on the MLS. This means that, regardless, your opportunity for exposure is mostly on a level playing field.

> If a franchise or an independent wants to keep the listing in house (not put it on the MLS), it's a disadvantage for the seller.

Advantages of Franchises

Large franchises have other advantages:

- *Transferees.* This is perhaps their biggest advantage over independents. It's the same type of advantage that national airlines have over smaller regional airline companies. The nationals can feed into the local franchisee buyers who are transferring from one part of the country to another. In other words, if you're selling your house in Boston through a nationwide franchise, and moving to Los Angeles, you'll be recommended to a local Los Angeles franchise of the same company. There's no way an independent can compete with this. As a result, if you're a seller who has a house that's likely to be a target of a transferee, you'll be doing yourself a disservice by not listing with a national franchise.

- *Advertising.* Larger firms often can afford to advertise more. Plus, they have the advantage of name-brand recognition. That means that buyers are more likely to seek them out. And that means more buyers come to see your property.

- *Standardization.* This is both a plus and a minus. With a large national franchise, you can be assured that the forms used and the procedures followed will be well thought out and designed, hopefully, to protect both the agent and you. On the other hand, the agent is likely locked into those procedures and forms and cannot help you as easily if you have a special need.

Advantages of Independents

Independents have their own plusses:

- Chances are the independent has to be twice as good in order to survive in today's competitive market. (Either that or so bad at selling, no franchise will hire the agent!) If you see an active, independent office, chances are it has hard-working, on-the-dime agents.

- Independents can sometimes do a better job in meeting your demands. If they choose, they can cut their commissions or accept a second mortgage in lieu of immediate payment, without having to contact a central office, which is likely to say, no, based on company policy. They can mold their advertising to fit your property's needs, rather than fit you into institutional advertising. They can tailor their service to fit your individual needs.

A Tough Decision

As I said at the beginning, I always try to choose the person over the company. However, depending on my needs and the property I have to sell, that can be a hard decision.

> Whether you choose independent or franchise, always choose a *local* agent. An agent who is more than just a few miles away from the property can never really service it well.

Power Tip 8
Make Sure the Agent Has a
Sales Plan

If you want to get from here to there, from "A" to "B", it helps to have a plan. I can remember once sitting in an office with an agent and a seller. The seller, who was pretty savvy, said, "So, you want to list my property. If I give you the listing, what will you do to sell it?"

The agent gave her best smile and said, "I'll put up a really big sign in front. Everyone who comes by will see it and call. It will sell."

The seller said, "A sign is nice, but what else? What about an advertising campaign? What about having other agents tour the property? Aren't you already working with buyers who are looking? Can't you bring them by?"

The agent smiled her best smile and simply nodded. She'd do some of that, too.

Needless to say, she didn't get the listing. The seller was asking the agent to spell out exactly the steps that would be taken to sell the property, and the agent was being vague and uncertain. Would you have listed with her?

Why Agents Don't Like to Give You a Plan

The above story illustrates several points. First, some agents don't have a clue as to how to sell your property. Second, agents who do know often don't like to be held to a specific set of parameters. You as a seller, however, are entitled to know the agent's plan.

The reason agents don't like to tell you their plans is that they know from experience that there is no real way to say in advance just where a buyer will come from. Their plan may be to give the property as much exposure as possible and hope for the best.

A typical agent can handle half a dozen listings at any given time. As the number of listings goes up, the agent's ability to give them all the needed attention goes down. If an agent tells you he or she has a dozen or more listings, you have to question whether that agent will really have time to give yours the attention it needs and deserves.

Therefore, even good agents simply don't know where the buyer will come from, and they don't like to be pinned down to telling you exactly how they'll sell your house.

A Poor Plan

On the other hand, realizing that sellers want to know, some agents will tell you what your want to hear. They may even hand you a brochure explaining their approach.

Selling Your House—A Poor Sales Plan

1. Put sign in front.
2. Advertise your specific property in local newspapers.
3. Hold at least three Open Houses.
4. Bring all current buyers (working with agent) to see the house.
5. List on the MLS and the Internet.

The preceding sales plan has at least three areas (2-4) that are probably a waste of time for you. Of course, they could turn up buyers, but statistically they are a long shot.

For example, it's very rare that agents would have a buyer waiting in the wings to buy. Yes, they may be working with many buyers, but the chances that one of them would decide to buy your house, out of the thousands offered for sale, is actually remote. They need to find your buyer.

In addition, agents know that advertising a specific piece of property is usually a waste of money. Agents' ads are designed to draw in buyers and sellers (whose properties they can list). Once in, the agents will attempt to sell those buyers your house. Statistically, however, a buyer who phones in on an ad for a specific house almost never buys it!

Even holding a public Open House, something many sellers insist upon, as noted earlier, is not a technique that's likely to sell your house. Studies have repeatedly shown that the prospects who stop by an Open House almost never purchase that house. Thus, a public Open House may not help you much.

Yet, as a seller, you may find the symmetry and the ideas appealing. However, except for a sign and listing the property, the agent hasn't put forth any specific techniques to realistically move your property.

What Kind of a Plan Should You Expect?

I like an agent to be up front with the facts of selling real estate. I like it when an agent says, "The only way to really sell your house is for me to expose it to as many buyers as possible. I don't have any magic formula or plan. The truth is that it's simply a numbers game. Get enough buyers to see the house, and one of them will want to buy it."

Then I like the agent to spell out how he or she is going to get that exposure. In addition to putting up a sign and listing the property (the minimum necessary), I like to hear the following things.

Selling Your House—A Good Sales Plan

1. The agent is going to bring other agents by to tour the property on more than just one occasion (caravaning).

2. There will be several agents' Open Houses (not open to the public) to help get the word out.

3. The agent will "talk up" the property at regular agent meetings.

4. The agent has a regular schedule of advertising (not necessarily my house) which will bring in potential buyers.

5. The agent has access to transferees coming in from out of state who might like to buy my house.

6. He or she will contact the transfer department of local corporations to see if they have anyone interested in my house.

7. The agent will call at least once and usually several times a week to update me.

> It's important that the agent not only let you know his or her plan of action, but also keep you well informed as to its progress. Constant communication keeps you on top of what's happening and let's you know that things are moving forward, even if no buyer has yet come forward.

Thus, a good agent's plan is really nothing more than a moving strategy. It aims at getting you maximum exposure, whatever that takes, for as long as it takes to find you a buyer. Couple that with the other requirements (a fixed-up house, a good price, reasonable terms, and so on) and you should soon have a sale.

3
You Can Save on the Commission

Power Tip 9
Save on the Commission

Everything in real estate is negotiable, including the agent's commission. Furthermore, although at first it may not seem like it, different agents charge different commission rates. Simply by shopping around, you should be able to find an agent who will sell your property for less.

> In a hot market where properties sell quickly, the perceived need for a full-service agent is greatly reduced. As a consequence, more than I've ever seen before, agents recently are discounting and lowering their commission rates.

No Standard Commission Rate

It's important to understand that real estate agents cannot set a rate that all must follow. Rather, the rate of commission is determined by each agent in cooperation with each seller.

This is not to say, however, that agents won't tell you what their rate is and refuse to budge. This may be particularly the case with large franchise companies.

For example, an agent may say that his or her rate is 6 percent. If you ask if that's negotiable, you may get a polite, "No, it's not. I know what my services are worth, and I charge accordingly. If you want to pay less, you'll get less, and you're probably better off with someone else."

Some sellers take this as a starting position for negotiations, sort of like trying to knock down the price in an open-air bazaar. That's usually a mistake. An agent who expresses a certain minimum fee and tells you to take it or leave it may indeed be giving you her bottom line. She really won't work for less, and if you want to pay less, you will have to go elsewhere.

> If an agent says he or she won't take less than a certain percentage in commission, you should respect that position. If you want to pay less, you'll simply have to look for another agent.

Why Won't an Agent Cut the Commission?

The simple reason is that, *from the perspective of the agent,* commission rates are low and expenses are high. It's important to understand that, in real estate, it's rare for an agent to get the entire commission. Rather, it's divided up between agents and their offices. A typical split might look like this:

Typical Commission Split (6 percent)

To seller's agent	1.5 percent
To selling office	1.5 percent
To buyer's Agent	1.5 percent
To buying office	1.5 percent
	6 percent

Of course, not all splits are like this. Sometimes the seller's or buyer's agent gets more, perhaps 2 percent. Sometimes the buying office gets more than the selling office. It all depends on what's customary in the local area. However, on a 6 percent commission, your agent probably gets only 1.5 to 2 percent. The only big difference would come about if he or she not only lists your house but also finds the buyer. Then the agent could get 3 to 4 percent.

On the other side, your agent has many expenses that he or she must absorb. These include the following items.

Typical Agents' Costs

- *Auto and car expenses.* As you've certainly noticed, agents require a relatively new, upscale car in which to cart buyers around. Yes, any car could do, but most people like to feel that they're with a successful agent, and a fancy car helps that image. All of which means a significant cost for the agent.

- *Insurance.* Agents must carry "errors and omissions" as well as heavy auto and office liability insurance to protect themselves and you. Sometimes their office provides it; sometimes they must pay the cost themselves.

- *Clothing.* Agents are constantly meeting people, and they must "dress for success." You'll never (or almost never) find an agent coming to your door in jeans and a sweatshirt. Most will dress up in suits and other appropriate attire. Yet another expense.

- *Signs, business cards, stationery, and so on.* Sometimes the office pays for this; sometimes it's the agent's expense.

- *Phones.* An agent's phone bill can run into the thousands of dollars a month. This includes landlines, cell phones, and secretaries to answer phones.

- *Advertising.* Often the office pays for this. But some agents will spend their own funds advertising their listings.

- *Other expenses.* Agents hold open houses for other agents and will often provide refreshments for those stopping by. They will produce flyers with color pictures of your house to give away. There are dozens of small services such as these that agents provide and pay for.

It all adds up. However, the biggest expense that's not listed here is time. The agent spends his or her time on your listing. And unless there's a sale, the agent does not get paid a nickel for it.

> The flip side of this is that sometimes the property sells almost instantly and the agent spends very little time on the sale. From the agent's perspective, however, this all balances out among many listings. From your perspective, if yours is the property that sells quickly, a big commission may seem like little value for so much money spent.

Thus, many agents are very reluctant to reduce their commission rates. They feel, with some justification, that, given their expenses, they are getting little enough as it is!

Why Would Some Agents Cut Their Commission?

On the other hand, you will probably find agents who will agree to a lower commission. Instead of 6 or 7 percent, they may agree to list your property for 4, 4 1/2, or 5 percent. Why would they do this? Aren't their expenses just as those high as for full-commission agents?

Yes and no. As in any profession, some people are more efficient than others. They make more with less.

Also, some agents are basically listers. They sign up as many listings as they can and then hope that other agents will sell the properties for them. They don't advertise or promote your property, hence their costs are less. They may accept a 4 1/2 percent rate from you, for example, and offer the selling agent 3 percent. They aren't getting much, but then again, they aren't doing much, either.

Finally, some agents are discounters. They do provide some services, but hope to make up in volume what they don't make on each individual sale. We will cover all of these in the following tips.

Shop Around

The bottom line is that when it comes to the commission, there are all sorts of different rates out there. Unless you happen to be in a particularly cold market, check out at least four different agents. Get recommendations from friends. Drive around neighborhoods and look for signs to see who is most active in the area. Check to see which offices are advertising in the local papers. As a last resort, check the phone book. Look for agents who have been around the longest. (In some Yellow Pages, the company advertising the longest often gets the first placement. In others, it's the size or the ad that determines location.)

Then, simply ask what their minimum commission rate is. You might get some pleasant surprises.

Power Tip 10
Be Sure a Cheaper Agent
Will Do the Work

Whether you're paying full rate or less on the commission, you want
to be sure that the agent you hire is going to do the work. If the work
is going to be split between you and the agent, be sure you're very
clear on what you're to do and what the agent will accomplish.

When you're working with a broker who is working for a lower
commission, very often much of the work involved in selling the
house is left for you to handle. There's nothing wrong with that, as
long as you're aware of it up front.

> One of the biggest problems that occurs between sellers and
> brokers who charge less is over who does what. Frequently, the
> seller believes that the broker should do everything, even
> though the commission has been cut. The broker, on the other
> hand, believes that with less money comes fewer services.

What Is Required to Sell a House?

It's important that you, as a seller, have a good sense of what's really
involved in getting a house from the point where you've made the
decision to sell to closing escrow and transferring title to a buyer. A
list of what's involved is on page 39. (We've already discussed some
of these in detail and will discuss others as we go.) Of course, not
each item will apply to every transaction. But more than likely most
of the items will apply to your transaction. Check which task the
agent will perform and which is up to you.

What Are the Biggest Tasks?

That really depends on how savvy a seller you are. For most sellers
who aren't all that familiar with real estate transactions, there are
three really hard parts:

- Showing the property to strangers
- Writing offers and handling paper work
- Managing the escrow

This doesn't mean that you can't get in trouble with some other chore. It's just that these three tend to be the biggest hurdles for most sellers. Therefore, it's usually a good idea to make sure that the agent will handle them. Here's a more complete task list.

Tasks in Selling Your House

	Agent	Seller
1. Fix up the property	☐	☐
2. Put a sign in front	☐	☐
3. Create and disperse flyers	☐	☐
4. Advertise the property in newspapers	☐	☐
5. "Talk up" the property to agents	☐	☐
6. List the property on the Internet	☐	☐
7. Promote the property elsewhere	☐	☐
8. Show the property to buyers	☐	☐
9. Provide information on schools and crime	☐	☐
10. Provide information on houseowners' associations	☐	☐
11. Analyze up offers to buy	☐	☐
12. Negotiate offers and counteroffers	☐	☐
13. Check with an attorney for legal advice	☐	☐
14. Open escrow	☐	☐
15. Provide disclosure statements	☐	☐
16. Do repairs as required	☐	☐
17. Clear title	☐	☐
18. Manage the escrow	☐	☐
19. Resolve disputes as they occur	☐	☐
20. Close the deal	☐	☐

Will the Agent Show the Property?

A full-service agent most certainly will. This agent is touring would-be buyers to many houses, and if the buyers seem interested and qualified to purchase yours, the agent will bring them by. The agent will usually call first to make sure you're home and if not, will use the "lockbox" on the house to gain access.

A selling agent who is willing to accept a lower commission very often will simply call to let you know that buyers are on their way over and that you should show them the house. Indeed, you may not even have a lockbox on your house.

On the other hand, assuming you're paying a reasonable buyer's agent's portion of the commission, you can expect the buyer's agent to go through the motions of calling first and showing prospective buyers through your house.

Will the Agent Write Up Offers and Handle Paperwork?

All full-service, full-commission agents perform these tasks. Lower-rate agents, however, may only do some of it, such as writing up the offer. You might be in charge of handling disclosures.

Disclosures are an important part of every real estate transaction. Some are required by national edict, such as lead in the home disclosures. Others may be required by state law. And yet others you will want to disclose to protect yourself against a buyer later coming back and claiming you covered up something that was wrong with the property. Check Chapter 8 for more information.

If you're not familiar with the home-selling process, you will want to be sure that your agent handles *all* the paperwork for you, even if you have to negotiate a higher commission rate. On the other hand, if you're a savvy seller, you may want to handle much of the work yourself.

Will the Agent Manage the Escrow?

Managing the escrow means that someone (you or the agent) follows the escrow process making sure that any liens against your title are cleared up, the buyer is making good progress toward getting a loan, and all problems are dealt with in a timely fashion. You need an escrow manager to be sure that everything gets done in a timely fashion so that the deal can close on schedule.

A deal that doesn't close on time may simply fall apart, you could lose the sale.

Managing the sale requires that you know what needs to be done and when. If you're not an expert in real estate transactions, you're really better off letting an expert handle this for you. See also Chapter 10.

How Do You Negotiate the Work Load?

It's important to remember that the essence of negotiation is give and take. If you want something, you must give something else up in return. If you want the agent to do all the work of the transaction from beginning to end, then be prepared to pay for it. You'll probably end up paying a full commission.

On the other hand, if you're willing to do some of the work, then expect to be compensated for your time and effort. Expect to pay less to the agent.

You will need to find an agent who does not adamantly stick to a policy of full commission or no listing. You need to find an agent who will work with you—compromise and allow you to do some of the work for some of the commission.

Don't make the big mistake of thinking that there's no work to be done. There's lots of work involved in closing even the simplest real estate transaction. If no one does it, then the deal simply won't close.

Power Tip 11
Try Listing with a Discount
Fee-for-Service Broker

A discount broker is one who advertises up front that he or she will accept listings at lower than the going rate. (Remember, there is no "set" rate. The "going rate" is what most agents in the vicinity are charging.) There's no need to argue about lowering the commission here. It's a given.

Discount brokers tend to be most active in hot markets. Recently, markets in Seattle, Denver, San Jose (Silicon Valley), and elsewhere have seen a spurt of discount brokers.

How Do I Find a Discount Broker?

They advertise their services in usual and, sometimes, not so usual ways. I've seen flyers distributed door to door. I've seen newspaper, TV, and radio ads. And, of course, there are the ubiquitous Internet ads. (Usually, the Internet advertising is to draw people to web sites, which because of their incredible proliferation are otherwise hard to find.)

As of this writing, I have not seen any of the major national franchise companies come out pushing discounts. However, that's certainly a possibility as long as the market remains hot.

What Do They Charge?

The fees vary enormously. Usually, these brokers are "fee for service." That means that they tell you what you'll get and how much it's going to cost. Sometimes there's a fee schedule for different things you might want the broker to do.

For example, a basic listing of your property on the MLS might cost you between $500 and $1000. Of course, you'd still be liable to pay a commission (typically 2 1/2 to 3 percent) to the agent who brings the buyer by.

> Note: On the east coast real estate attorneys have long done the basic services in a house transaction (documents, searches, escrows, and so on) for between $500 and $1500 The only thing that's new here is that now real estate agents are beginning to offer the services they perform at a similar discounted price.

I've seen other brokers offer to do basic services for anywhere from $50 to $500 for drawing up an offer to $50 to $100 for handling disclosures or inspections. Some will manage your escrow for a fee, while others will charge you for the sign in the front (typically $50 to $75) and for flyers (sometimes a free service used to get you in the door).

What Do I Get?

Quite frankly, you get what you pay for. In a fee-for-service arrangement, what you get should be quite clear—if you pay $50 for a sign, that's what you get. With a simple listing, you should ask the agent to spell out exactly what services (in addition to a listing on the MLS) you're getting. There may be several or none.

> Be sure that you're actually dealing with a broker or a salesperson working for a legitimate broker. Anyone offering to sell your house for you must be licensed. This usually includes having several years of experience as well as passing often rigorous exams.

Should I List with an Online Service?

This can be confusing for many people. When you list your house on the MLS, you may also be automatically listing it with an Internet listing service such as www.realtor.com, which is affiliated with the National Association of Realtors and has arrangements with many

MLSs to put their listings online. However, many brokers in addition to (or sometimes instead of) listing your house on the MLS will also put it up on their own web site.

Having a house on a web site can be an advantage. But you should be aware that, to date, relatively few houses are sold as a result of listing them on web sites. Most buyers still do it the old fashioned way—through agents and the MLS.

> The MLS is an agents' listing service. Normally, only Board members (usually Realtors®) put listings on the MLS and have access to online and print books showing current listings. This is almost a moot point, however, since most of the MLS listings are already on services such as realtor.com.

There are some brokers, however, who specialize in listing your house both on the Internet and on the MLS. For example, home-bytes.com has been offering to do both in selected areas of the country for around $500. They do this by having affiliated brokers in those areas handle the listing for you.

Another company, ehome.com has recently been advertising that it will list your house on the MLS for you. However, my observation is that their fee structure tends to be higher and more complex.

As time goes on, many more similar services will become available. In addition, expect specific fee-for-service agencies to crop up and begin to advertise in most areas.

Will You Still Have to Pay a Buyer's Agent?

It's important to understand that we are talking here about the *seller's portion* (usually half) of the commission. You still would need to pay a commission to the agent who finds you a buyer. As previously noted, this is typically $2^{1}/_{2}$ to 3 percent. Thus, your costs are whatever the discount broker charges you to list your house *plus* whatever else you need to pay the buyer's agent.

But, you may be wondering, can't you get a discount on the buyer's agent's fee as well? If the seller's agent will do it for as little as $500, won't the buyer's agent do it for that little as well?

Probably not. You can offer to pay the buyer's agent less. But remember, buyers' agents are scanning the listings looking for houses to sell to their clients. What do you think they'll do when they come across two similar properties, with the big difference being that one seller is offering a full 3 percent buyer's commission and the other is offering 1 percent? What would you do?

> In theory, agents are required to show their prospective buyers the most suitable houses, regardless of what the commission may be. This, however, isn't what always happens in actual practice.

How Do I Know a Discount Broker Is Reputable?

Check them out the same way you would any other businessperson. Ask for references and *call* those references. Ask them how long they've been in business, how many listings they have, and their percentage of sell through. Ask for the MLS numbers so you can check out their figures. Even better, get a referral from a friend, associate, or relative.

4

Sell It Yourself

Power Tip 12
Sell Your House by Yourself

The only way to save a whole commission when you sell your house is to sell it by yourself. That's called selling For Sale by Owner (FSBO). While no hard statistics are available, it is widely guessed that about 15 percent or more of all houses are sold in this fashion.

Can you really sell your own house without the aid of an agent? It's certainly possible. As just noted, hundreds of thousands of people do it successfully each year. On the other hand, that doesn't mean it's easy, or that after considering what's involved, you'll want to do it.

How Much Can You Save?

The amount to be saved can be quite staggering, depending on how you figure it out. For example, let's assume a commission rate of 6 percent and a selling price of $200,000. At first glance, that seems to be a savings of $12,000, not an insignificant amount.

> Many people feel that they are willing to do a considerable amount of work when they see the size of commission they'll save. However, just looking at the rewards can skewer your judgment. You also have to consider the work involved.

Many people, particularly those involved in promoting FSBOs for one reason or another, argue that this is really a deceptive figure. The reason is that even though the commission rate is based on the sale price, most people, in reality, don't own their properties outright. They actually have a relatively small equity. For example, if you're selling your house for $200,000, chances are you don't own it free and clear. Indeed, you might only have $50,000 or less in the property.

If you're paying a $12,000 commission on a $50,000 equity, that means that the actual rate (based on equity, not sales price) is roughly 25 percent! In other words, selling through an agent is going to cost you nearly a quarter of the equity in your property!

Looking at it that way causes many more people to seriously consider going the FSBO route. Indeed, it often makes believers out of skeptics.

You Have to Do the Work of Selling

As I said, the other side of the coin is the work. You can't let the rewards blind you. You must also consider what you'll have to do to earn them. Here's a short list of the tasks involved in selling your own home.

The Work of Selling Your Own home

1. Fix up the property (which you'll have to do in any event).

2. Get a sign and stick it in the front yard.

3. Arrange and pay for newspaper advertising.

4. List your house on free services on the Internet (described in the next tip).

5. Hold your own "Open House" (if you want). This means allowing anyone who shows up to go through you home.

6. Go to local companies and solicit the help of their transfer departments.

7. Create an advertisement to go on a public access channel of a local TV station.

8. Create flyers and put them out on your "For Sale" sign, in grocery stores, and on other bulletin boards.

9. Be home at all times to catch phone calls from potential buyers. Yes, you can use an answering machine, but buyers often won't leave their name and number. You need to talk to them directly.

10. "Sell" your house over the phone when buyers call.

11. Show your home to those buyers who do call. Remember, nobody but you is screening these people. And there are some criminals out there who could make it a point of checking out FSBOs for future robberies and worse.

12. Negotiate directly over price and terms when you find a buyer.

13. Handle the paperwork which includes:
    - A sales agreement
    - Disclosures
    - Settlement documents

- Inspection reports
- Escrow opening and closing instructions

14. Obtain a termite clearance. (The buyer won't be able to obtain financing without it.) Also, you'll need to arrange for any termite repair work.

15. Clear the title to your property, in case there are any liens or encumbrances that need to be removed.

16. Manage the escrow.

17. Deal with the buyer's anxieties and problems during the closing period.

18. Let the buyer have a "final walk-through."

19. Handle a buyer who wants or needs to pull out of the deal after the agreement is signed.

20. Move (which you have to do anyway).

The idea behind this list is not to scare you away from selling your house on your own. Rather, it's to show you the many different task involved, some of which many people find distasteful, even potentially dangerous. Most people, in fact, have some hesitations when it comes to letting perfect strangers walk through their homes.

Many people, when they actually see what they have to do to sell their property on their own, begin to think that maybe that agent's commission isn't as much as they thought, after all!

Are You Really Up to It?

That's the important decision. Can you do it? You certainly can try. Do you want to do it? That's another decision.

It's important to understand that I'm not trying to make that decision for you one way or the other. I'm not trying to push you into selling on your own by emphasizing the rewards or scare you away by pointing out the tasks involved. I'm simply trying to let you know what's really involved so you go into it with your eyes wide open.

My best advice is this: If you're even remotely considering saving the commission by selling FSBO, then go ahead and try it. Only set a rigid time limit. You'll give it a month, or 2 months, or whatever. If after that time you haven't sold the property or you're disenchanted with attempting it, you give up and list with an agent.

Setting a time limit and trying to sell FSBO for a while will ensure that you won't wake up nights afterward wondering if you could have saved all that money by just trying to do it yourself.

Power Tip 13
List It on the Internet

The name of the game when selling your own house is exposure. And one way to get lots of exposure is to list your house where as many potential buyers as possible will see it.

Of course, the best listing service is the MLS that Realtors® use. However, listing there means that you're going to have to pay a commission. (It's not clear that you must necessarily pay a commission to list on the MLS. However, how many agents do you think will bring potential buyers to see your house if you don't offer to pay a commission?)

The next best are the various other listing services that are available. These are all on the Internet. As of this writing, I counted over a dozen major services. There could be hundreds. The point is that the largest and most well hit (seen by those searching for houses) are going to be your best bet.

Keep in mind, however, that as of this writing, even the best FSBO services are quite limited when compared, for example, to www.realtor.com, which offers most MLS listings and claims to have over a million listings at any given time. If an FSBO site has 100,000 true listings, it would be an enormous marketing accomplishment.

What Should I Look for in an Internet Listing Service?

If you're going to list on the Internet, you should be selective. Here's a list of priorities you will want to consider:

FSBO Site Requirements

1. *The listing should be free or inexpensive.* If you're going to have to pay a lot of money, you might as well list with an agent.
2. *The listing site should be very active.* You want a site that lots of buyers visit; otherwise, why bother to go through the hassle of listing?
3. The site should allow you to put up at least one image of your house.

The old adage, a picture is worth a thousand words, applies here. If buyers see and like the looks of your house, they are more likely to take the time to read the listing details.

4. The site should give you enough room to list all the important attributes of your house. That includes at least the following:
   - Square footage
   - Number of stories and style of house
   - Number of bedrooms and bathrooms
   - Size of lot
   - Location of house
   - Amenities such as fireplace, den, spa, pool, and so on
   - Special terms, such as seller financing.

   If you're allowed to list more, all the better.
5. The site should allow you to also list with an agent on the MLS.
6. *The site should help you with the transaction.* For example, some sites provide signs, hints on selling, tips on advertising, even copies of some of my books!
7. *The site should link you to associated services.* These include mortgage companies (which you can recommend to buyers), title and escrow companies, and so forth.

What's the Maximum I Should Pay to List My House on a Web Site?

As just noted in number 1, you should find sites that are inexpensive or free. However, you may want to pay for specific services provided. For example, if the site provides you with a good-looking sign that you can stick in the ground in front of your house, it's not unreasonable to pay $50 or so for it. After all, that's at least what you'd pay to have it made up yourself, and the site is saving you the hassle. Plus, it will probably look better than one you buy in the hardware store.

On the other hand, for providing you with specific ads that you can use as well as tips on selling, you probably wouldn't expect to pay much. That should simply part of the site's information program.

Some sites require that you pay a nominal fee up front when you list, often under $25. However, when you sell, they charge an additional amount, as much as $500. I would seriously consider whether the site provides enough benefits to warrant paying that much money either up front or at the end of the transaction. After all, what if you find a buyer who didn't come to you through the site?

Are you still obligated to pay? How does the site know the buyer did not contact you first, and then you suggested that the buyer take a glance at the site listing?

> The real weakness of web sites that want to charge for a successful sale is that they have limited means of finding out if you sell. Most don't have the resources to check county records. If you don't tell them and don't used any of their financing services, chances are they won't know! Hence, the big up front fee.

What Are Some Good FSBO Sites?

Here are some sites that I have found to be helpful. Keep in mind, however, that FSBO sites come and go, and their services change. Be sure to check out thoroughly any site you are considering.

FSBO Sites

Owners.com. As of this writing this seems to be the largest of the FSBO listing sites. It will allow you to put your house up for sale for free for 1 month. For either $99 or $299, you can get a longer listing and other services which include virtual tours.

> A company called IPIX has developed a technology that allows it to transform just a few images taken of your house with its special camera into a three-dimensional tour. If you haven't tried it, check out some of the web sites that offer virtual tours. You'll be amazed!

Yahoo.com. Yes, this is the famous Yahoo portal. They also have a real estate classified section where they will list houses for free. However, if you list your house on owners.com (mentioned previously), you will find that it's automatically listed on yahoo.com as well. The advantage of listing with Yahoo.com is that it is one of the most heavily trafficked of all web sites on the Internet.

Aol.com. AOL also offers classified listing for free. However, on several occasions when I tried to look at those listings by owner, I could not find any. You will need to check this out on your own.

homebytes.com. This service charge a fee of around $500 to list your property both on its home site as well as on your local MLS. It does this by having licensed brokers work with it around the country. It is one of the more successful FSBO sites.

Power Tip 14
Pay an Agent or Attorney to
Handle the Paperwork

In talking with many sellers who did sell by owner, and others who would have liked to, the biggest area of concern I heard expressed had to do with the paperwork. A real estate transaction involves lots of legal documents. And most novice sellers just don't feel up to handling that. They don't feel qualified, and they're afraid that if they make a mistake, not only could it cost them the deal, but it could also land them in a lawsuit. From that perspective, paying a commission could seem cheap!

There is a way, however, to have your cake and eat it, too. That's to pay only for those legal services you need, in this case writing and handling documentation. You may want to perform all of the other services involved in selling your house (advertising, showing the property, and so forth) yourself, but just don't feel at ease with the paperwork. Then why not do the rest of it yourself, but hire an expert for that part with which you're not comfortable.

Whom Can I Hire?

If you're on the east coast, it's easy. There are real estate attorneys almost everywhere who either specialize in home sales or who handle it as a hook to get other business in the door. The typical fee for their services is anywhere from a low of about $500 to a high of around $1500. It's interesting to note that this fee structure hasn't changed much over the past 50 years, and, as such, represents an enormous legal bargain!

In the rest of the country, real estate attorneys are harder to come by. And regular attorneys may charge fees that are very significantly higher. However, the good news is in these other areas real estate agents often handle the entire transaction.

Today, in order to enhance their incomes as well as to bring more business over the transom, many real estate offices have begun handling fee-for-service document work. They will charge so much to write up the sales agreement. Handling disclosures is a certain amount. Handling closing documents another fee, and so on. For complete documentation, fees range from a low of about $1000 to a high of around $2500, depending, of course, on the agent.

> Keep in mind that agents are not attorneys and are not sup-posed to do any legal work. That, however, doesn't seem to stop them from drawing up sales agreements.

Agents or attorneys who do your paperwork assume a certain amount of liability. If something isn't done right, they know you'll be back to complain. Consequently, they normally carry costly errors and omissions insurance to protect themselves, and this expense is usually passed on to you.

How Do I Find a Fee-for-Service Agent or Attorney?

Most advertise. Check the Yellow Pages of the phone book, the real estate section of your local newspaper, and web sites on the Internet. When you check the Internet, be sure you look for local people. You don't want to be dealing with an out-of-the-area agent or attorney. Being close by is a definite asset.

Who Really Should Do Which Documents?

You can, of course, have either an agent or an attorney handle all of the documents. However, certain paperwork is better handled by one or the other.

> The safe answer is to always have an attorney do all of the paperwork. In theory, you're thus getting legal advice, which an agent cannot give you. However, in actual practice, I've found many agents who handle offers and other documents on a daily basis are much more familiar with the work than some attorneys who handle it only on an occasional basis.

What Is the Paperwork Involved?

Here are some of the documents involved in a transaction and the person who is likely to give you the lowest price as well as good service. Remember, it's a good idea to always have an attorney review all documents before signing them in any transaction.

Paperwork in a Transaction

1. *Purchase agreement (also called "sale agreement" and "deposit receipt")*. This is the document on which the buyer makes the offer. By signing it and agreeing to its terms, you make the sale.

While, of course, an attorney should always review this document for legal concerns, an agent is probably your best bet when involved in negotiations. The agent should know how to deal with buyers and what to include that's most likely to get both what you want and a successful deal.

2. *Disclosure statements*. This is the document you give to the buyer which tells what specific features you have in the house (such as a dishwasher, air conditioner, pool heater, and so on) as well as what defects, if any, exist.

Again your best bet here is a real estate agent. Agents deal with disclosures all the time. If you have something you're not sure about, you can ask the agent. He or she should be up on what must be disclosed.

When you are in a quandary over whether or not to disclose something which might be a defect, my advice is always to disclose it to the buyers. Chances are it won't affect the sale. On the other hand, by making full disclosure, you help to protect yourself from the buyer later coming back and claiming you concealed something. Check into Chapter 8.

---

3. *Reports*. These include termite, professional house inspection, soil, and other reports. Some you will pay for (such as the termite report). Others the buyers will pay for (such as the professional house inspection).

Your best bet here is an agent. The agent can help you interpret what the report means in the context of the sale. Sometimes a bad report will require renegotiating the sale with the buyer, and an agent can help here, too (probably for an additional fee).

4. *Removing title clouds.* These are liens or encumbrances that prevent you from giving clear title to your property. They can be anything from an old unpaid debt to a boundary dispute.

You can probably handle much of this yourself. But for bigger problems, you will probably want to consult with an attorney.

5. *Escrow and closing statements.* You will have to sign instructions when you open escrow and closing statements before you can get your money out and close the deal. While an agent can help explain some of the costs involved, if there's a problem involving title, you will want to speak to an attorney.

Power Tip 15
Get Agents Working for You
When You Sell on Your Own

When selling your house on your own, it's useful to think of it as list-ing it with yourself. If you "list" your house with yourself, you are less likely to forget that you have the lister's responsibility of getting the word out and of doing all the work involved in the sale.

Also, as the lister, you also have the option of "cobrokering" with "other" agents. In other words, you can share your listing.

Of course, some sellers rebel at this because it means they'll have to pay a commission, and their entire goal in selling by owner is to avoid the commission. For those who feel that way, it's worth remem-bering that your true goal should be to sell your house for as high a price, and as quickly, as possible. If that involves bringing agents in, so be it.

> It makes little to sense to take longer to sell and to accept a lower price by refusing to work with agents. Better to pay a part commission for a quicker, higher sale.

Why Work with Agents?

As we note elsewhere in this book, agents have the system in place to find buyers for your property. If there are 1000 agents working in your area and each one knows half a dozen potential buyers, by plugging into the agent network, you immediately have access to up to 6000 potential buyers. Further, chances are that almost every buyer in your area is currently working with one agent or another. You would be fool-ish to ignore this giant selling machine ready and in place to help you.

How Do You Get Agents to Work
for You?

The trick, of course, is to get agents working for you without paying a listing commission. The answer is to pay a buyer's agent's commis-sion, which is roughly half. If a full commission is 6 percent, a buyer's agent's share is usually 3 percent.

But as an FSBO, how exactly do you work with a buyer's broker? What do you sign? What kind of commitment must you make?

The first thing you must do is to let buyers' agents know that you're willing to work with them. This can take many forms. Some FSBOs will put a small sign right on the big "For Sale" sign on their lots saying, "Will Cooperate with Brokers." This immediately lets any agent driving by know that you're willing to pay a buyer's broker's commission. Since any agent driving by is likely looking for a client in your area, it's a good way to start.

You may also indicate in any advertisements that you're willing to "cobroke." Use that word and agents will know exactly what you mean.

As discussed in Chapter 3, you may want to consider using a discount broker to get your house listed on the local MLS. However, this will inevitably cost you some money in addition to what you will have to pay a buyer's agent.

Finally, as soon as you put your FSBO sign out in the front yard, expect to get calls from agents who want to list your property. Tell them that you're willing to cobroke and will pay a buyer's agent's commission, but that you don't want to list.

Many agents who call on an FSBO don't have a buyer for your house. They really want to list it. You have to separate the wheat from the chaff here. You, presumably, don't want to list, but you will cooperate on a sale if the agent has a buyer. Be sure that you always make that perfectly clear to any broker who calls.

> Beware of agents who say they have a prospective buyer but really don't. Some agents have been known to traipse relatives and friends through FSBO homes in the hope of duping the sellers into signing a listing agreement. Be sure that any buyers an agent brings by are real, as evidenced by a legitimate offer.

Should You Sign a Listing Agreement?

No agent with even half a brain will bring a buyer to see you until you've signed a listing agreement. Otherwise, you, on your own, could simply strike a deal with the buyer and leave the agent out. This means, therefore, that in order to work with a buyer's agent, you'll need to sign some sort of listing agreement. But what kind?

The answer is that you want to sign an agreement that commits to you paying a half commission to the buyer's agent only for producing a buyer who's ready, willing, and able to purchase. That's only fair.

You don't want to sign a commitment that allows the buyer's agent to treat you as a listed property and then go fishing for buyers. That's tantamount to signing a standard listing agreement. Therefore, you need to know the different types of listing agreements.

Different Listing Agreements

- *Exclusive right to sell.* You must pay the agent even if you sell the property yourself. This is the standard agreement, and not something you want as an FSBO.
- *Exclusive agency.* You must pay this agent no matter what, even if another agent brings in a buyer. In other words, you agree to deal only with one agent. (You don't pay a commission if you find the buyer yourself.) Again, this is too limiting for an FSBO.
- *Open listing.* You will pay a commission to any agent who brings in a buyer. You're not limited to dealing with one agent, and you are not committed to paying a commission if you sell the property yourself. This is usually the right listing type for an FSBO.

> The listing agreement will specify exactly what type of listing it is. It should also spell out your commitment in terms of when you will pay a commission and how much you will pay.

It's important to understand that no agent worth his or her salt will accept an open listing and do any work on it in terms of finding a buyer. The agent understands that time, money, and effort put forth could be wasted because you could sell through another agent or by yourself.

However, if the agent *already* has a buyer, it's a different story. Then, by signing an open listing, the agent helps to ensure that you'll pay a commission, *if* that buyer happens to be the right one.

What If the Agent Insists on an Exclusive?

An agent may call you up one day and say, "I've got a buyer for your house. But, I'm afraid to waste my time bringing her by because you're working with other agents. I'll only bring her by if you sign an iron-tight agreement, an exclusive listing."

What should you do?

First off, realize the agent does have a point. It's very hard to collect a commission on an open listing. If another agent claims he or she showed the buyer the house first, or if the sellers say they showed the house to the buyer first, the buyer's agent may need to go to court to get it straightened out. It's much easier for an agent to collect on a tighter listing.

What I'd do, if I thought that agent had a legitimate buyer, is agree to the agent's demands for an exclusive agency listing or even for an exclusive right-to-sell listing. However, I'd only give it for just 1 day. For that 1 day, for example, that agent would have the exclusive right to sell my property. He or she could feel fully protected. But, if the buyer that the agent brought by didn't purchase that day (or later on—typically buyers are locked in for 90 days after they are shown the property), then I'm back on my own.

Note that if another agent or even you, yourself, found a buyer and signed a sales agreement during that day, you could owe a commission to the agent to whom you'd given the 1-day exclusive right-to-sell listing. So be careful!

> The term of a listing agreement is fully negotiable. It can be for as long as a year (or longer) or as short as a single day.

Don't be hesitant to offer a 1-day listing. It may be something new to you, but buyers' agents who deal with FSBOs are fully aware of it.

Power Tip 16
Offer Creative Financing

As an owner/seller, you may be in a position to beat out the competition by offering financing incentives to potential buyers. After all, if you're saving on the commission, you may be more inclined to give a little on the financing.

What Is Creative Financing?

The term *creative financing* became popular a few years go when it was relatively difficult to get institutional loans for many borrowers. As a buyer, unless you had sterling credit, you just couldn't get financing and that meant you couldn't buy a house.

To offset this situation, many agents began suggesting that sellers offer to carry the loan. The seller would give the buyer "paper," usually a first or second mortgage or some combination of the two and, with this financing, the buyer could complete the purchase. Because it wasn't the traditional financing from a lender such as a bank or an S&L, it was called *creative*. In truth, it was nothing more than seller financing.

How Does It Work?

It's really the essence of simplicity. Instead of getting cash from the buyer, you get a mortgage (actually a note and trust deed in most states). Usually, you receive payments each month, interest on the unpaid balance, and a due date, typically 3 to 5 years off, when it all gets paid off. All the paperwork can be quickly drawn up by the escrow/title insurance company.

The rub, of course, is that instead of cash, you're getting paper. If you're in a position where you can afford not to get all your equity out in cash, then it's easy. But, if you need the cash, for example, to purchase another house, then it's more difficult.

A big problem with lender financing is the risk. If the buyer doesn't make the payments and defaults on the mortgage, you must go through foreclosure to get the property back. The foreclosure process, however, could end up being so costly that it's easier to take a loss on the paper! That's a good reason to look for only credit-worthy buyers.

The Buy-Down

Another form of creative or seller financing is the *buy-down*. Here the seller pays the lender points (a point is 1 percent of the loan amount) up front in exchange for giving the buyer a lower interest rate. A lower interest rate allows the buyer to more easily qualify to get the loan and makes purchasing the house easier.

A buy-down is most often used by builders to help lower the barrier to potential homebuyers. However, it can be used by any seller.

How Can I Do a Buy-Down?

There are two ways. If you already have a buyer who had a lender but for some reason is having trouble completing the deal because of problems qualifying, you can volunteer to buy-down the mortgage. It's a technique to use when the deal would otherwise collapse.

Another way is for you, as a seller, to go out and find a lender. Get an appraisal and a commitment to loan on your property to a qualified buyer. Then, offer to buy-down the interest rate on the loan to the lender.

Each point (equal to 1 percent of the loan amount) you agree to pay the lender will lower the rate. It generally costs roughly about one point for each $1/8$ percent reduction. To get a $1/2$ percent lower interest rate could cost you around four or five points.

You can advertise that you're offering to buy-down the interest rate. This will be an attractive feature to many marginal homebuyers.

Saving Money on a Buy-Down   With a buy-down, you're actually paying cash out of pocket to a lender to help lower the buyer's interest rate and, as a result, monthly payments. Why not compensate for this by increasing the price? (That's what many builders do.)

For example, you were offering to sell for $250,000. Now you agree to buy-down the buyer's loan by $1/2$ percent for $5000, but you boost your selling price to $255,000. You get the same amount of money, but the buyer gets a lower interest rate. It might just be the incentive a marginal buyer needs to purchase your house.

> You can't always raise your price. Remember, your house must appraise out by the lender. Sometimes lenders will go with a higher price if you have a buyer in hand ready to pay it. Other times, they'll balk. A lot depends on what the lender's appraiser comes up with. Of course, if you don't like the appraisal, you can always ask for another or switch lenders.

When Should You Use Creative Financing?

If you're in a hot market with buyer's offers coming at you from all angles, you obviously don't need to worry about creative financing. On the other hand, if the market has cooled down and you can't seem to get buyers to make offers *or* if interest rates are high and buyers are having trouble qualifying, it's time to play the creative financing card.

Remember, every time that interest rates go up $1/2$ percent, you eliminate tens of thousands of potential buyers from the market—people who would otherwise like to buy your property but simply can't afford to get in.

> Anything you can do to make your house more attractive than the one for sale next door will increase the likelihood of a faster sale. One good method is to make your financing more attractive.

How Can I Protect Myself?

Any time you consider creative financing, the issue of seller protection comes up. In the case of helping finance the buyer, it's increased risk. In the case of a buy-down, it's increased cost. How do you insulate yourself against the risks and the cost?

If you're considering lending the buyer the money to purchase your house, you should do the following:

Safeguards for Carrying Back Financing

- *Ask for a three-bureau credit report.* It's what the banks do, and it will only cost you about $50. Further, the buyer will probably pay for it! The three main credit bureaus are: Experion 800-682-7654, TransUnion 800-916-8000, and Equifax 800-685-1111.

> Be wary. Most sellers are blinded by their need to sell. If the credit report turns up problems, especially previous foreclosures, turn down the buyer. Better that you don't sell than you sell to a bad buyer and lose all your equity later on.

- *Confirm the buyer's employment.* You want to see consistent, long-term employment with a salary more than high enough to make the payments. As a general rule of thumb, if the buyer doesn't make three times the monthly principle, interest, tax, and insurance payments, don't sell to him or her.

- *Confirm the buyer's assets.* Never agree to 100 percent financing. Always insist the buyer put down at least 10 percent plus any closing costs. This is to protect you from a "rip-and-run" buyer. Confirm the buyer's assets by a letter from his or her bank. (A *rip-and-run buyer* is one who puts up no cash, buys the house, rents it out collecting all the rent and making no mortgage payments, and then runs when you finally foreclose.)

Notice that what you're doing here is nothing more than what an institutional lender would do. It's just being cautious.

5

Dress the Property
to Sell

Power Tip 17
Fix Up Your House before
Showing It

If you want buyers to drool over your property and offer you top dollar, then you have to show it in its best light. And that means doing some work. If you're not planning to fix up the house before you sell, then don't expect to get the best price in any market.

Whenever I tell people this, I tend to get resistance (unless, of course, the house is truly a dog). They may say that they are wonderful owners, keeping their property up so that it's a showcase. Why, any buyer would have to be crazy not to see the value there.

Baloney! If that's what you're thinking about your property, forget about it. *Every* property that's being lived in needs some work. The very act of living in the house runs it down. When it's time to sell, you need to have your property evaluated in terms of its appearance, and then you need to fix it up so it shows well.

> Don't show your property until it's all fixed up. If you do, you're likely to get low-ball offers, perhaps from buyers who would have offered more if they had seen the property in tip-top shape.

Who Can Evaluate My Property?

All real estate agents can give you an opinion, often a highly accurate one since they look at properties day in and day out. You don't have to list with them to get this opinion. Just ask them what they think you should do to make your property more salable. They'll tell you.

You can also have an architect and a landscape designer come by and give you their opinions. If you pay them, it shouldn't cost more than a couple of hundred dollars apiece, well worth the money. On the other hand, they may simply come by and give you a free estimate in the hope that you'll hire them as part of any work that you do.

Don't be surprised if you find out that there's extensive work needed to put your house in shape. It's true of nearly every house.

Should I Do the Work?

It depends on how committed you are to getting top dollar and a quick sale. If you're going for the gold, you have to pay the price, and that usually means doing some fix-up work.

Of course, keep in mind that you can usually do most if not all of the required work yourself. No one is saying you have to hire gardeners, painters, plasterers, carpenters, and so on to get your house in shape. Rather, over the course of several weekends, you may be able to do a lot of what's required yourself.

> The hardest part usually comes from living in the house during the same time you're trying to fix it up. If at all possible, try to arrange to stay at a friend's or relative's place during the heavy workdays. It will make things go faster and help you keep your blood pressure down.

What Sort of Work Will Be Required?

That, of course, depends on the condition of your house. However, most houses need at least the following, all of which will be covered either here or in the following tips:

Fix-Up Work Usually Required

- Landscaping, particularly of the front yard and any other area visible from the street
- Cleaning or redoing the driveway
- Painting and refurbishing the front of the house
- Painting throughout the house, inside as well as out
- Putting in new carpeting
- Fixing up problem areas such as kitchens and baths
- Fixing any other area of the house that looks bad

What Should I Do First?

If you're building a house, usually the landscaping comes last. You certainly wouldn't put in a lawn and shrubs before excavating because the construction work would ruin the landscaping. Similarly, if you're doing a makeover, you'd wait until the renovation work was done before putting in the yard.

However, presumably here you're not building from the ground up or renovating. (If you are, check into my recent book, *Tips & Traps When Renovating Your Home*, McGraw-Hill, 2000.) You're just fixing up the house to get it ready for sale. Consequently, there shouldn't be any heavy construction work that will ruin the landscaping.

On the other hand, time is always an issue. When it comes to landscaping, there's a definite trade-off between time and money. For example, if you have the time, you can seed a front lawn and wait 3 months for it to come in, all for a cost of under $100. On the other hand, if you need to have the lawn up in a week, you can call the gardeners to plant sod and it will be up and green, at a cost of many thousands of dollars.

The same holds true for all planting. If you have the time, you can plant and wait for mother nature to do her miracles. Flowering plants can blossom in a month or so. Roses can be flowering within several months. Bushes and trees, of course, tend to take longer, depending on what size they are when you purchase them. Of course, all of these things can be done in a few days if you're willing to pay to have mature plants, shrubs, and flowers put in.

> With landscaping, it's always a trade-off between money and time. If you leave yourself enough time, you can save a bundle of money.

This, of course, is the reason why I suggest doing the yard work, the landscaping, first. It's not because it's more convenient. It isn't. It's because you can get the most bang for your buck by spreading the work out over time. Rush it and you'd better have a thick wallet.

Coordinate Your Efforts

Having said that you should do the landscaping first, it's important to temper that comment with some common sense. If you need to paint the exterior of your house, don't put flowers or bushes in right where you're going to paint. Paint first, then add the bushes. But that shouldn't stop you from going ahead with the lawn and other areas where painting and similar work won't affect planting. And certainly it shouldn't affect any trimming, which can be handled immediately.

Remember, there are three steps to getting started in fixing up your house

Steps to Getting Started Fixing Up Your House

1. Get your property evaluated to determine what fix-up work needs to be done. (Don't allow yourself to be your only evaluator.)

2. Determine exactly what you'll need to do.

3. Get started right away with the landscaping.

In the following tips we'll look at other areas you should work on, in the order in which you should get to them.

Power Tip 18
Paint and Clean Everything
First

The quickest, cheapest, and easiest way to fix up a house for sale is to clean it and paint it. I realize that cleaning and painting may not be your cup of tea. It's not mine either. Nevertheless, if you want to get the most bang for your buck, this is where to do it.

Nothing says "look at me!" more than a fresh coat of paint and cleaned carpets. They show off your house in a better light and make it more appealing to buyers. In truth, you cannot afford to put your house up for sale until you've painted it and cleaned it!

> As noted in the last tip but well worth repeating, it's a good idea *not* to show your house to any potential buyers, until it's fixed up. First impressions are critical and form the basis for assessing value. Anyone who sees your house messy and dirty will remember it that way, even after it's cleaned up, and will offer less. Wait a few weekends until you can get your place shined up to show it, and you'll get more money for it in the long run.

Can I Do It Myself?

Certainly. All it takes is paint, brush and roller, cleaners, and some will power. You can do your entire house inside and out for just a few hundred dollars, tops. However, the better question is, should you?

Assuming that you have some equity in your house and are going to get cash out of it when you sell, it probably will pay you to have a professional paint it. It always pays to have a professional clean it.

In today's market, you can have your entire house painted inside and out for around $3500 (for around 2000 square feet). If you want a quickie "slap and dab" job, it's closer to $1500. A real pro might charge $5000.

The point, here, is that painting is not particularly expensive, when you compare it to the other building crafts. And, when you consider that you will almost certainly add far more than the cost of the painting to the value of your house, it usually makes sense to have a pro do it.

Besides, painting is messy work. Do it yourself and spill a can of paint on your carpet and you've just lost your profits in carpet replacement. Besides, unless you are quite good at it, it's hard to get a really fine paint job.

Cleaning, on the other hand, is just plain hard, dirty work. But, you can usually hire a cleaning crew to come in for a day for a few hundred dollars and spiff up your entire house, especially kitchen and bathrooms. They will probably do a much better job than you can; they have the chemicals and cleaners to do it right, and they are fast. And having a pro clean your carpets (check Tip 20 to see why putting in new carpets may be a better idea) is the only way to go. To my way of thinking, there's never a good reason to do the cleaning yourself. (You can even tell your spouse who's worried about saving money that I said so!)

What Exactly Should I Paint?

The tip says "paint everything." That's not much of an exaggeration. But you can go overboard. I can remember walking into a condo a few years back where the owner made a deal with a painter to do it all. The painter covered up the windows and floor, then came in with a spray gun and painted everything in sight, including walls, ceilings, doors, woodwork—you name it!

The problem was the painter used all the same paint, a flat finish. Yes, it certainly looked clean. But, it also looked weird. Most of us like to see the trim (doors and woodwork) in a washable high-gloss finish in a complimentary color. The same holds true for the walls and ceilings in bathrooms and kitchen.

> While you should paint everything, you also need to do a good job.

Pay special attention to the front of the house. This is the part that potential buyers first see. Remember, you never get a second chance to make a good first impression. You want the front of your house to sparkle.

In particular, give the front door several coats. It's what would-be buyers first see up close. If the door looks good, they will assume the rest of the house looks good, too.

If you have the funds, put in a new hardwood front door. They cost around $1000—2000, but they say "elegance" about your house.

Next, pay special attention to the entranceway. It's the would-be buyer's first glance inside your house.

Then, paint the ceilings. Most people think they can skip ceilings because they don't have marks on them. That's usually a mistake. While ceilings don't normally get scuffed up, they do get dirty over time and appear darker. That darkens the rooms and makes them appear drearier. Put a fresh coat of paint on the ceiling and it will liven up the whole room.

Next, paint the kitchen and bathrooms in a high-gloss finish and be sure to do a good job. Would-be buyers look closely, here.

Finally, paint all the walls. While you may simply overlook scuffs and marks that are there, would-be buyers won't.

Warning: Don't try to wash paint that's more than a year old. Don't ever try to wash "flat" paint. You'll just create smears, and the demarcation between new and clean and old and dirty will make the whole thing look bad. Scrubbing flat paint simply takes it right off.

What Colors Should I Use?

Surprisingly, that's not your choice! Remember, you're fixing up to sell, not to live in. Thus, you must use colors that most people will find attractive or at least neutral.

Studies have shown that very light colors (avoiding greens, blues, pinks, and any other intense colors) are best. Typically, white is your best choice with cream coming in second.

Yes, these colors will show dirt the most. But you're painting to sell, not to live in. Once the buyers purchase the house, it's up to them to keep the paint clean!

When Should I Replace Instead of Paint and Clean?

There's a simple rule that applies, here. If it's broken, fix it. If it's not, paint or clean it.

Of course, there's also a lot to be said for obsolescence and the need to bring your house up to modern standards in order to get a high-value sale. We'll have much more to say about that in Tip 21.

Power Tip 19
Do Something about the
Driveway

For nearly all houses, the driveway is the biggest single feature of the front perspective of the property; it's what you see most of when you first drive up. As a consequence, the condition of the driveway forms a large part of the first impression of would-be buyers. Getting a solid, clean driveway, therefore, is a must when fixing up your house for sale.

I'm sure that many readers will question this. It's like saying that a doormat is important. (It is!). Isn't a driveway just something to park your car on? Who worries about driveways?

In truth, no one should worry about driveways. In fact, if your driveway is neat, clean and in good order, would-be buyers won't pay any attention to it, and that's as it should be. However, if your driveway has oil and rust stains on it, is broken, or otherwise has problems, would-be buyers will notice it, and that will color their impression of the property overall.

> A good driveway will only make a neutral impression on buyers. But a bad driveway will definitely create a bad impression of the property.

Does It Matter What Kind of a
Driveway I Have?

Yes and no. There's a kind of pecking order in driveways that speaks to the quality of the property. The order is roughly as follows:

Pecking Order of Driveways

- Brick or tile
- Concrete
- Asphalt
- Gravel

If your driveway is brick, it speaks clearly that yours is a quality house (assuming you haven't overbuilt the driveway for the norms of your neighborhood). On the other hand, if you've only got gravel, it says something quite different.

I'm not suggesting you should go out and get a new driveway—just that the quality of a driveway does make a difference. Besides, regardless of the driveway, you can do things to make it look better.

You can be sure gravel driveways are raked and that there are no weeds in the gravel. You can put a fresh coat of tar on a paved driveway. You can clean cement driveways. And you can be sure no bricks are out of order on a brick driveway.

How Do I Clean the Driveway?

That depends on what type it is. The easiest driveway to clean is asphalt because you can put a new coat of tar down. You can always hire someone for a couple hundred dollars or so to come out and put on it on (actually it's like a thick, black paint). It will make the driveway look brand new, at least for a few weeks.

> Tar driveways tend to get lots of cracks in them, particularly at the edges (called "alligator cracks" because of their appearance, which is similar to alligator skin). These cracks make them look old and worn. It's well worth the extra money to have new paving done, at least over those areas.

With bricks, you can often replace cracked ones and realign those that have gotten pushed out of place. Weed killer will usually handle any scattered weeds that have broken through. If you've got cement bricks (stamped), see below.

The hardest driveway to clean and fix up is cement. Assuming that there are no significant cracks (a significant crack is anything above a hairline and particularly one on which the cement is offset on either side), you will want to remove oil and rust stains. Oil stains usually come from old cars that leak from their engine. Rust comes from leaving iron objects on the driveway during wet periods.

Of the two, the oil stains are easiest to remove. There are many different compounds sold in auto supply stores that will get the oil off. I haven't found any one that's better than another, so just take your pick. Some heavy scrubbing also will help.

Rust stains are harder. They seem to penetrate concrete and the various compounds don't tend to get deep enough to get them out. Your best bet is to hire someone who has had experience removing stains. There are professionals listed in the phone book who can remove almost any kind of driveway stain.

I've had some success doing it myself with household bleach as well as with the type of acid used to adjust the pH of swimming pools. But be very careful with either of these. They can burn your hands and the fumes can be dangerous. *Never mix acid and bleach or other cleaners—the results can be extremely toxic!* Use gloves and follow other precautions found on the labels.

> Use of harsh chemicals to clean a driveway can result in "burning" nearby grass and shrubs. Take care to use lots of water to dilute the chemical before it reaches susceptible foliage.

Real problems occur when the cement driveway is cracked. Now you must decide whether to rip it out and put in entirely new cement or just work on a portion of the driveway.

Some creative solutions involve cutting out the areas of the cracks (assuming that the entire driveway isn't cracked) along parallel lines and then either recementing just those areas, or adding bricks as a decorative touch. Sometimes by staggering cement with bricks you can both fix and upgrade the driveway at the same time for a relatively low cost.

> Don't try to patch cracked concrete. It never works and it always comes out looking like a cheap solution.

Stamped driveways, which are actually concrete into which a pattern has been stamped (and sometimes a color added) are harder. They often crack, but not along the stamped seams. When that happens, it may be possible to cut out just the cracked portion, reconcrete and restamp it.

Fix Up Walkways, Too!

While the driveway is important, walkways leading from the driveway to the front door (or from the sidewalk to the front door) are also important. Nothing makes a worse impression on a would-be buyer than to stumble and fall over an uneven or broken walkway. It could even land you a lawsuit!

Needless to say, do all of the things mentioned earlier to walkways. In addition, be sure that any adjoining lawns, flowers, or other landscaping is neatly trimmed and doesn't flow over and onto the walkways.

Usually, it isn't necessary to replace the walkways. Only if they are very badly broken or if they never looked good to begin with, would I consider it. Sometimes, an inexpensive fix is to buy the large cement steps found at building supply stores. For around a hundred dollars (depending on length) you can use them to quickly lay a new and attractive walkway.

Power Tip 20
Get New Carpeting!

This is my plug for spending a few bucks when fixing up your house to replace, rather than just clean, your carpeting. I think this is money well spent, and as we'll see, it doesn't have to cost you an arm and a leg.

Why Are Carpets Important?

Most people, when they walk through a house, tend to look down. And what do they see? In most houses it's wall-to-wall carpeting; it's what makes the biggest impression. It tells them the condition of the house. (We'll talk about wood flooring shortly.) Good-looking carpeting speaks of a plush, upscale house. Dirty, worn, or torn carpeting says something entirely different.

So, how good is your carpeting?

Most people who have put in carpeting in the last 5 years think theirs is pretty good. But, is it really? The difference between carpeting that looks good and that which looks bad can be slight.

What Makes a Carpet Look Bad

- Stains of any kind, particularly spots and large dark areas.

- Worn areas typically found in high-traffic spots such as hallways and the entrance to rooms. These often appear after as little time as 6 months.

- Dark colors or unusual weaves. They may please you, but chances are they won't be appealing to most would-be buyers.

It's important to understand that even with the best-quality wall-to-wall carpeting, stains and wear can occur quickly, often within a year. While cleaning can help, it has a tendency to make the carpeting look even more worn, particularly if done several times. (Unless the cleaner is a professional who uses high-quality chemicals, you can actually damage a carpet by cleaning it!)

Therefore, my suggestion is that if your carpeting looks at all bad and cleaning doesn't bring it back to an almost new appearance, replace it.

New carpeting, even very inexpensive new carpeting, adds immeasurably to the quality feel of a house.

What about the Cost?

A friend of mine recently recarpeted her house. The cost was $15,000. Am I suggesting you spend that much on carpeting as part of your fix-up prior to sale?

Hardly!

You can replace all the wall-to-wall carpeting in most houses (around 2000 square feet) for about $3500, often much less. And the new carpeting will look lush and appealing, at least for a year or so.

It's important to understand that unlike most other products for the house, new technology has allowed the price of many carpet products to go down, instead of up. Today, there are many fine carpeting products out there that cost significantly less than they did 10 or 15 years ago.

Further, if you're doing a whole house for resale in a typical neighborhood, it's not necessary to get the very best quality. What you want is primarily something that shows well. And today you can get that for not a whole lot of money.

If you're in an upscale neighborhood where the norms are $100 a yard for carpeting, you'd be wise to spend the bucks on superior flooring. After all, if you expect to be getting $500,000 or more for your house, you'll expect to spend a few bucks to get it to look like its neighbors.

Use a Carpet Broker

One of the best-kept secrets in real estate is that you can buy carpeting at almost wholesale prices if you're not too particular about style or color. Today, there are carpet brokers in most areas who will come to your house with a limited number of samples. You pick what you want. The broker orders the carpet from the factory and arranges for a crew to install it. (It might be the same crew that the local department store uses to install carpeting!)

You pay near wholesale prices. Remember, the broker doesn't have a showroom or any inventory. That means a dramatic price reduction, sometimes as much as half or more off store prices!

You can find carpet brokers listed in the phone book. However, a better source is to contact a local real estate company that handles rental property. If it handles a lot of rentals, it surely is replacing carpeting on a regular basis. And if it does so, it's undoubtedly using a carpet broker. Most agents would be happy to pass the information along, with a recommendation, to you.

What Color and Quality Should I Choose?

Go with near white or a very light beige. Is this a color I would suggest for anyone to live with? Never! You have to take your shoes off just to keep from getting dirt on it every time you walk across the floor.

But for showing, nothing works better than a light color. It makes the house look luxurious, large, well appointed. And, you can ask would-be buyers to take off their shoes when they visit. While you might think this is a turn-off, it actually is the opposite. It emphasizes that the carpeting is new and clean, and it makes the house look less like a resale and more like something brand new!

As for quality, choose something that's appropriate for the quality of houses in your area. Usually, a nylon plus works well, but any carpeting that's got a tight weave will do. Remember, even very cheap carpeting, when it's brand new, usually looks terrific.

What If I've Got Wood Floors?

Many houses don't have wall-to-wall carpeting. Instead, they have wood flooring with throw rugs. This is particularly the case in the midwest and parts of the east coast.

Nothing looks richer than the warm tones of a wood floor that's in good shape. Nothing looks worse than a wood floor that's scratched up and pitted (remember how old schoolroom floors used to look?).

All of which means that you should put your wood floors into shape. For real wood, that means a light sanding and then restaining and new coats of varnish or other floor finisher. Yes, this can cost a few bucks, but it's usually much less than to buy wall-to-wall carpeting as noted earlier.

If the floors are not too bad, sometimes you can get by with just a sealer/stain and polish. Try it to see how it comes out, first. You can always sand it down.

If you have a synthetic wood floor (such as Pergo), keep in mind that it only looks like wood. Sand it and you'll ruin it.

Rather, there are a variety of solutions and polishes that you can use to bring back the original luster. Be very careful with burns. These may require replacement of a portion of the flooring.

Power Tip 21
Fix, Don't Replace

Almost inevitably, when it comes time to sell and you begin inspecting your property, you'll find something that's broken or in such bad shape that it might as well be broken. You realize that in order to sell, you're going to have to do something significant (read "expensive") to get rid of the problem.

> Don't think you can hide significant problems. These days almost all buyers will wisely insist on a professional inspection, which will probably turn up the problem. Besides, if you know about it, you should disclose it to the buyers, or else they might come back at you after the sale with demands that you fix it, on their terms.

Here's the best advice you can get. Whenever possible, fix, don't replace. This will save you money in both the long and short run.

What Kinds of Problems Can I Expect?

It really depends on how old your house is and on its condition. Older houses will have more serious problems than newer ones, mainly because owners tend to defer maintenance. The longer it's deferred, the more problems will crop up.

Here's a short list of some of the more common problem areas that house owners discover, once they begin looking, along with the price for fixing and replacing.

Costs of Possible Problems

Problem	To fix (patch)	To replace
Leaky water heater	Can't be fixed	$500
Leaky roof	$500 to $1500	$5,000 to $15,000
Broken furnace	$200 to $1200	$2,000 to $3,500
Broken air conditioner	$200 to $1000	$1,000 to $3,500
Leaking pipes (whole house)	$100 to $400	$5,000 to $7,000
Bad wiring (whole house)	$100 to $500	$3,000 to $7,000
Cracked foundation	$1000	$15,000 to $????

From this list, it should be clear that there's an enormous price difference between fixing (patching) and replacing. Usually, fixing will cost you only a fraction of what it will cost to replace.

Why Not Replace It?

Many of us are from the old school. We don't believe in putting a band-aid on a wound when stitches are needed. We like doing a job the "right" way, totally, completely, and finally. I have no argument with those of you who feel this way. Actually, I feel that way about most things myself.

However, when you're getting a house ready to sell, there are two big reasons that you should fix instead of replace:

It's important to understand that the purpose of fixing is *not* to conceal the problem. You should disclose to potential buyers both that the problem existed and how you chose to remedy it if you want to avoid costly buyer's complaints later one.

1. *Usually, the buyers won't be able to see the work that you've done.* Replace a furnace, and who's to know? Replace all the leaking water pipes, and it won't show.

Replace all the wiring in the house, and not one sign of it will be visible.

In most cases, the work you do simply won't be demonstrable to potential buyers. And buyers won't pay for that which they can't see.

Yes, you can point out that you've just spent $2500 on a new air-conditioning system. You know what the buyer's likely reaction is going to be? They'll say (or think), "Great, you should have spent the money since it's your house and you should maintain it. But don't expect me to pay 10 cents more in price because you've done work that you were supposed to do!"

Anything you have to point out to a buyer that's normally hidden, such as new wiring or plumbing, simply isn't going to get you a return on your money. In other words, it's deferred maintenance that you suddenly have to pay all at once. It comes out of your equity. It's less cash you'll receive from the sale.

But, you may note, some things do show, for example, a new roof. Won't buyers see that? Yes, they will, which brings up the second reason to fix and not replace.

2. *Buyers may not like your replacement choice.* Your composition shingle roof leaks, so you replace it. Except the buyers want wood shingles. Or they want tile.

You've got a tile roof, so you replace it. Except you put on blue tiles and the buyers prefer red. Or you put on red, and they prefer blue. Or you put on the cheapest tile roof you can find, and they want a more expensive roof.

Get the idea? If you're the one who's going to live on the property, it's easy to satisfy yourself. If you're going to sell, you've got to satisfy someone else. And you won't know that person's tastes or desires until they make an offer you can accept on the property. And that's normally after you get the property spruced up for sale.

> You are normally only required to offer a roof that doesn't leak (assuming you don't sell "as is")—not a new roof. You only need a heating/air conditioning system that works, not a new one. And so on.

What If the Buyers Complain about the Fix-Up Job?

Of course, any savvy buyer is going to ask for a professional inspection of your property. And the inspector may point out that although you've "fixed" the problem, it is likely to recur. For example, you may patch a roof. However, if the roof is old and worn, new leaks may occur during the next rainy season. Or you may have fixed an old furnace, but the motor may break down the next time it's put to heavy use. Or you may have closed all the leaks in the pipes, but if they're rusted (as in galvanized piping), new leaks are likely to occur.

The buyers may point out that (because of the inspection report or your disclosures) the problem has only been temporarily fixed. It needs a total fix. In other words, they want a new roof (or new heater or new piping or new whatever).

If this happens, and it may, it's time to negotiate. You can point out to the buyers that you're not giving them a defective house. At the time of the sale, everything does, in fact, work or not leak.

However, if they're concerned about future problems, then you're willing to work with them on it. A new roof may cost $15,000. You'll give them $5000 off the price toward the new roof. They can put it on after they buy the house and pay the rest of the cost themselves.

Note the difference here between replacing and negotiating. If push comes to shove and you must do some replacement work to close the deal, you probably will only end up paying a fraction of the cost. You'll end up splitting it with the buyer. If you take it upon yourself to do the replacement work before you have a buyer, you'll end up footing the entire bill.

> In many areas, recent markets have been very hot with many buyers, few properties, and escalating prices. In such a market, you may feel you can simply refuse to negotiate any replacement work with the buyer, believing if this buyer doesn't take the house, another soon will. Just be sure of the market before you take this stance and chance losing a solid buyer!

When in doubt while getting your house dressed up for sale, fix—don't replace. You'll save money and be happier for your decision.

Power Tip 22
Don't Renovate to Sell

Some houses need renovation. Yours may have an old-fashioned kitchen, or bathroom, or your house may be too small and need an extra bedroom, or may have a terrible back yard, or. . . . You get the idea—there's something lacking in the house that can only be fixed by doing major renovation work.

Should you do it? Should you spend the money doing the renovation before you sell?

The answer, in general, is no. The reason is that most renovation work won't return you dollar-for-dollar spent. In other words, if you spend $10,000 doing the renovation, you may only get $5000 more on the sale. That means that you'll actually *lose* $5000 of your equity by doing the renovation!

Keep in mind that we're talking strictly about doing the work as part of fixing up your house to sell. It's a much different story if you intend living in the property for some time. In that case you'll get enjoyment out of the renovation work yourself, a totally different situation.

Of course, that's the general rule. The specifics in your case may be different. It all depends on where you do the work (closets, kitchen, garage, etc.), how necessary it is to the house, and how good a job you do.

Work You Should Never Do in Order to Sell

There are certain renovations that simply won't get you your money out. These include the following:

- *Closets.* Don't spend a lot of time and money fixing up and organizing closets. You can spend thousands here. Buyers will thank you for it, love you for it, but not pay you a dime for it.

- *Shelves.* Your house may be lacking in bookshelves, entertainment centers, even extra kitchen shelves. These are expensive to add but return little to nothing at sale.

- *Room additions.* These are the most expensive renovations of all. You could easily spend $20,000 to $50,000 or more adding a den, bedroom, extra bathroom, and so on. Your chances of getting your money out, however, are slim.

> There's always an exception to every rule. Some additions may be necessary in order to sell your house for a good price. For example, if all the houses in your area have two bathrooms and yours only has one, adding that extra bath may not only get you back dollar for dollar but also much more because you'll be able to command a higher price overall for the house.

- *Pool addition.* Today an in-ground pool can easily cost $25,000 to $50,000. It's certainly a nice feature, one which buyers will enjoy. But, it's doubtful that you'll recoup your money when you sell.

Work You Might Do before Putting Your House Up for Sale

On the other hand, there are a few renovations that break the rules and just might get you back as much as you spend or more and which you should at least consider doing as part of your getting ready process.

- *Renovate the kitchen.* If your house is more than 30 years old and the kitchen has never been renovated, consider modernizing it as part of your fix-up-to-sell process. A total kitchen renovation can cost upwards of $50,000 or more. But a minor renovation might only cost $10,000 and could make an enormous difference in the presentation of your house. If your house is less than 30 years old, an even more minor renovation in the kitchen may help.

- *Renovate the bathroom.* Like the kitchen, the bathrooms are areas that buyers scrutinize. Old-fashioned tubs, showers, sinks, cabinets, and countertops say, "I need work." Buyers will discount what they think it will cost them to renovate, often much more than what it will actually cost you.

- *Renovate the lighting.* Older houses often have dark corners. Sometimes, a simple fix is to stick a lamp into the corner and turn it on when showing the house. Other times it may be necessary to actually put in a new window, skylight or artificial lighting. While this can be fairly expensive ($100 to $10,000 depending on the work done), the brightening effect can often earn every penny back and more.

How Do I Decide What Work to Do?

There are at least three factors you must consider when determining what and how much to renovate, if at all:

1. *What are the neighborhood norms?* If every other house in your neighborhood has granite or Corian® countertops in the kitchen or bath, consider putting them in your house as well. The buyers coming to see your house will expect it and will discount your house if you have, for example, old tile. Similarly, if all the other houses have whirlpool tubs in the master bathroom, consider putting one in your house as well. It's hard to overbuild if you just bring your house up to neighborhood norms.

2. *What is the age of your house?* If your house is 30 years old or older and it hasn't ever been renovated (or it's been 20 years since the work was done), it needs renovation. If you don't modernize, buyers will heavily penalize you in their offers.

3. *What are the market conditions?* Your chances of recouping the money you spend on renovation, indeed of making a profit, are in direct relationship to the market conditions at the time you sell. In strong markets where there are lots of buyers and few houses, most buyers want, indeed expect, the house they are buying to be in top shape. After all, they're paying top dollar. In a hot market you stand a much better chance of recouping your money.

On the other hand, if the market's cold, if there are lots of houses for sale with few takers, then any renovation at all may be a mistake. In a cold market, buyers are looking strictly for bargains. Anything that adds to their cost is a turn off, and that especially includes renovation work. You're far less likely to recoup your money, let alone make a profit, in a down market.

> Be loose with your renovation money in a hot market. Be tight in a cold market.

Can I Deduct Fix-Up Costs?

You may be able to deduct some fix-up costs done to your house within 90 days of sale. However, with the liberalized rules regarding capital gains on houses, this may be a moot point. Most sellers can exclude up to $250,000 per spouse of their gain when they sell. Check into Chapter 11 for more information on this.

If you're considering fixing up your house prior to sale, I suggest you check into my book, *Tips & Traps When Renovating Your Home*, McGraw-Hill, 1999.

6
Demand a Big Deposit

Power Tip 23
Demand a Big Deposit

The deposit isn't called "earnest money" for nothing—it shows just how serious the buyer is. The deposit is, presumably, what the buyer is risking should he or she fail to go through with the transaction. The bigger the deposit, presumably the bigger the risk to the buyer and, more likely, the more secure the deal to you.

That, at least, is the theory. In practice, it's not quite that clear. As a seller, it's unlikely that you'll get the deposit if the deal doesn't go through, unless it's very clearly the fault of the buyer, which it often is not, nevertheless, a big deposit suggests an earnest buyer.

> Remember, your goal is not to collect a deposit from a broken deal; your goal is to sell the property, and a big deposit helps ensure a successful deal.

On the other hand, from the buyer's perspective, you might be the kind of seller who likes to collect deposits from broken deals. This means that the buyer is going to be hesitant to put up a lot of money, unless he or she is pretty darn sure the deal will go through. Again, a big deposit tells you that you have a serious buyer.

How Big Is a Big Deposit?

It's not so much the actual cash amount as it is the percentage of the deal. If the buyer puts up 1 percent ($2000 on a $200,000 offer), it's a fairly small amount of money. If something backfires, the buyer might simply be willing to walk away from the deal, with so little at stake.

> *Note:* The buyer stands to lose *more* than just the deposit. If the buyer pulls out of the deal without a good reason, you, as the seller, could sue the buyer to complete the deal (specific performance) or for damages. However, most sellers do not do this because of the hassle involved.

On the other hand, if the buyer puts up 10 percent ($20,000 on a $200,000 offer), it's far more substantial. Few buyers are going to turn their backs on that much money.

The idea is to get as big a percentage of the offer in a deposit as possible. In most deals you will be lucky to get a 5 percent deposit.

Who Gets the Deposit?

The good news is that the deposit belongs to you, the seller. The bad news is you haven't a prayer of laying your hands on the money. Any savvy buyer will insist that the deposit be placed in escrow.

The reason is that buyers are wary that if the deal falls through due to no fault of their own (for example, you can't deliver clear title) and you have the deposit, you might not be in a position to give it back. You might have spent it and not have the money! Or you might be angry and refuse to return it, meaning they'd have to go to court to get the deposit back.

> Buyers who insist their deposit go into a seller's agent's fiduciary account are playing a foolish game. You're—the person the money is being held for—and if you demand the money from the agent, at least in theory, he or she must give it to you!

Hence, the deposit almost always goes to a neutral third party. Yes, it's your money, but don't count on it until the deal closes.

Why Would the Buyer Not Forfeit the Deposit?

In the old days, a real estate deal was pretty much made the moment all parties signed the sales agreement. Today, it's a different story. Buyers automatically insert all sorts of contingencies, conditions that make the purchase subject to certain events or approvals taking place. For example, here's a list of contingencies that a buyer might insert into a typical purchase offer.

Common Contingencies
The offer would state that the purchase was subject to:

1. The buyer getting appropriate financing.
2. The buyer approving seller's disclosure statement.
3. The buyer approving professional inspection report(s).
4. The buyer getting clear title to the property.
5. The buyer approving any work done to the property as part of the sales agreement.
6. The seller getting a termite clearance.
7. Any other contingency that the buyer and seller agree to.

As you can see, the list of contingencies is long, and it often takes a long time to get them all fulfilled. While getting the buyer to approve disclosures might only take a day or two, getting approval of all inspections could take 2 weeks to 1 month. During that time, the sale is up in the air. If the buyer doesn't approve of the reports (or some other contingency isn't fulfilled), there is no deal, and the buyer could be entitled to have the deposit returned.

> Buyers want lots of contingencies in the deal to ensure that they'll get their deposit back if there's trouble. As a seller, you normally would want as few buyer contingencies as possible in order to lock the buyer in.

As you can see, closing a modern transaction largely involves removing buyer's contingencies until, at the last, the buyer is locked into moving forward on the deal. Only then can you be fairly sure that the deposit truly could be yours if the buyers don't close.

Even then, however, be wary. Remember, you don't hold the deposit in your hands. It's usually in the hands of a neutral third party. That party won't turn the deposit over to you until the buyer says it's okay. A nasty buyer could refuse to turn the deposit over until you actually go to court to force that to happen.

> The deposit isn't yours until the buyer (or a court) says it's yours. Of course, to be rid of you and the deal, many buyers will simply let the money go.

Should You Sign a Release to Get the Deposit?

Sometimes, buyers will insist that you sign a statement that you won't take further action (such as suing them for damages) if they release the deposit. Should you sign such a statement? (*Note* Such a statement may not be legally binding in some circumstances.) If you're asked to sign such a statement, ask your attorney for legal advice.

Here, however, is some practical advice. If you weren't really damaged by the deal, in other words, it just couldn't be made due to circumstances beyond anyone's control and you continued to live on the property during the escrow period, then why not go the easy route and just settle for the deposit?

On the other hand, if the buyer capriciously withdrew at the last minute, causing you to lose a substantial amount of money—for example, a deposit on a new house you were buying—then you may feel less gracious.

Be Wary of Big Deposits with Lots of Contingencies

Sometimes, particularly when the market's hot, buyers will try to impress sellers by coming in with a huge deposit. For example, you're selling your house for $200,000 and the buyer offers a deposit of $30,000, that's sure to catch your eye.

However, the other side of the coin is that the buyer might have sprinkled the offer with many contingencies. In fact, the offer may be no offer at all, but rather nothing more than the buyer trying to hold your house off the market while he or she decides whether to really get serious over it. Remember, you don't get the deposit until all of the contingencies favoring the buyer are removed, and even then it's doubtful.

> A smaller deposit with an offer with no contingencies is better than a big deposit with an offer filled with loopholes.

Be Sure the Deposit Gets Cashed

No matter who holds the deposit—the agent, escrow, or you—once the sales agreement is signed all around, be sure that the deposit check is cashed. You don't want to end up holding onto a buyer's uncashed check that has been stopped or that doesn't have sufficient funds to back it up.

Power Tip 24
Go for a Variable Deposit

Usually, a deposit tendered at the time an offer is made is fully refundable until you sign, and as we've seen, often for a long time after you sign. The reason is that the deal often contains many contingencies. If the buyer doesn't approve them as agreed, there is no deal and back goes the deposit money. (If you're not clear on this, reread Tip 23.)

However, at some point in every deal a moment of truth is reached when the contingencies are cleared and the deposit finally, truly is at risk. That's the moment when the buyer must decide whether to sink or swim, whether to move forward with the purchase, or cling to the last contingency (refusing to approve it), and back out of the deal.

Once you, as a seller, realize the nature of a modern real estate transaction, why not use it to your advantage?

In other words, it really doesn't matter how much the buyer offers to put up in a deposit initially, since that money isn't truly at risk until the buyer's contingencies have been removed. What's the difference if it's $10,000 or $1, if the buyer is fully entitled to get it back? Until it's finally at risk, it's simply fool's gold, phony money intended strictly to impress you.

So, instead of being foolishly impressed by a worthless deposit, instead why not put some teeth into it. This is how it can be done.

How to Structure a Variable Deposit

Since you really don't care how big a deposit the buyer initially puts up (in a typical deal with lots of contingencies), don't argue about it. If the buyer puts up $5000, go along. If the buyer puts up $1000, go along. (If the buyer puts up less than $1000 on any deal, it's usually considered "insulting" and suggests a frivolous offer which you probably should not accept under any circumstances.)

However, add a contingency of your own. Insist that once the buyers remove their contingencies (disclosure approval, professional inspection approval, get a formal approval from a lender, and so on), they will increase the deposit to 10 percent (or whatever amount you find sufficient) of the purchase price—a big deposit!

Consider the effect of such a contingency. The buyer can dawdle and worry about this or that. But, the moment major contingencies have been removed, it's time to fish or cut bait. The buyer must put some serious money into the transaction or back out of the deal. If the buyer puts up the bigger deposit, you can pretty well count on a done deal from then on. If the buyer refuses and backs out, well, at least you now know where you stand.

Typically, the major contingencies will be removed about 2 weeks into the transaction, so the buyer has that long to come up with a real deposit.

You can add your own contingency insisting that, until the buyer increases the deposit, you have the right to continue offering the property and to accept back-up offers. In this way you lose very little during this "back -out" period.

It Looks Good to the Buyer

Using a variable deposit sounds good to most buyers. While not really offering them anything at all, it appears to offer them the opportunity of waiting to come up with a big deposit until they've had a chance to completely scout out the property (check the disclosures and inspection reports). This will often have the effect of relaxing a timid buyer. The agent (or you, if you're selling on your own), can point out that the buyer will have very little at risk, initially.

You, as the seller, come across as very fair-handed. You also appear to have nothing to hide about your property. In short, asking for a variable deposit often can make an otherwise impossible deal come together. And, if you're really a clever negotiator, it can even result in your getting some concessions from a not-so-savvy buyer.

What If the Buyer Wants More Time?

Sometimes buyers will agree to a variable deposit at the time the sales agreement is signed, only to renege later on when it's time to put up the money. If the buyer is simply stalling and trying to buy more time, you're usually best off simply dumping the deal and moving on.

However, sometimes a buyer may indeed be sincere about purchasing your property, but is wary of putting up more money in a deposit. The buyer may be new to real estate transactions or may have some sincere concerns about the property. When this happens, it's time to negotiate.

If the buyer is new to real estate, it's a matter of education. Either you or the agent needs to explain to the buyer that a critical juncture in the transaction has been reached. Unless the buyer comes up with more deposit money, he or she will lose the transaction. If the buyer really wants the house, he or she will have to swallow any fear and move forward.

On the other hand, if the buyer has some serious concerns, these should be addressed. Is there a problem with the property? If so, identify it and come up with a method of correction. Money is a great fixer. You may want to sweeten the pot by offering to throw in a few thousand dollars to correct a problem, even one you see as insignificant.

> Sometimes you may get a deal moving again by offering to leave a few thousand dollars for a month or two in escrow after the deal closes. The money will be used to fix or otherwise resolve a problem (for example, a potentially leaky roof) that might arise. If the problem doesn't happen (the roof doesn't leak), you get your money back. If it does, the money is used to fix the problem. Either way, however, the deal closes.

What If the Buyer Offers to Put Up "Paper?"

You normally expect a deposit to be a check, which can then be cashed. But what if, instead, the buyer offers to put up a note? This is a promise to pay at some time in the future and, because it can't immediately be converted to cash, is called "paper." Should you accept paper?

That depends on the buyer, what the paper says, and how savvy a seller you are. If you're new to real estate and you want to be sure of a deal, get the cash.

On the other hand, if you're willing to gamble a little, then sometimes paper can pay off, in a big way. The reason is that since paper isn't as good as cash, often the buyer will sweeten the pot by offering to pay a higher price for your house.

How Do You Tell Good Paper from Bad?

There are two ways:

1. *Get a credit check on the buyer.* If he or she is rock solid, never missed a payment, never had a credit blemish, then I'd feel pretty secure accepting paper. On the other hand, if the buyer has to explain away all kinds of problems, be wary. I'd stay away from the paper.

2. *What is the paper for?* Is it simply a promissory note, a promise to pay you money some time in the future? That's usually not worth a great deal and in order to collect, if you even can, you might have to take the buyer to court. On the other hand, some buyers are cash poor, but instead have a lot of property, some of which they may own free and clear. The paper could be a mortgage (second trust deed, for example) on the seller's other property. In this case a quick appraisal and title search of the other property should reveal the buyer's equity and the value of the paper. It might be as good as cash!

If the paper is solid and you're willing to accept the inherent risk of any paper (the potential need to foreclose or go to court to collect on it), go for it. But be sure to get something in return, such as a higher selling price!

Power Tip 25
Consider Not Signing a
Liquidated Damages Clause

Most real estate sales agreements today contain a "liquidated damages" clause. While the wording differs, the intent usually is to keep you from suing the buyer should the deal fall apart through no fault of your own. By signing the clause, you may agree that the deposit becomes the entire damages.

Liquidated damages clauses are written in many different ways and can have different consequences, depending on how they are constructed. You should have your attorney check the clause in your document and explain its meaning to you. Our purpose here is to look at the clause from a negotiating, not a legal, perspective.

The usual advantage to you of signing is that should the deal fall through because of some fault of the buyer, you might more easily claim the deposit. Assuming the buyers also sign the clause, they have more or less written off the funds if they back out of the deal without cause. (There's not necessarily a guarantee that you'll get the money, however. The buyer can still assert that you're not entitled to the deposit because of some contingency and you still might have to take legal action to get the funds.)

The usual disadvantage to your of signing the liquidated damages clause is that if you are, in fact, damaged because, for example, you lose out on the purchase of another house and lose your own deposit, you normally can't sue for more than your buyer's deposit. Again, a lot depends on how the clause is written and the circumstances of the deal.

A Small Deposit and a Liquidated
Damages Clause

Some savvy buyers who want to tie up property for any number of reasons (they may be unsure they really want your house, they may not currently have the cash to buy, they may be hoping a better deal comes along, and so on) may offer you a purchase agreement that calls for a very small deposit and insist that you sign the liquidated damages clause. Beware of this situation.

The buyer, here, is trying to reduce his or her risk. As we've seen, a small deposit means the buyer has much less to lose. That small risk is further reduced when you sign the liquidated damages clause. Assuming it holds up, the buyer can then simply walk away from the deal at any time and not worry about you pursuing him or her for more money. You might get the deposit, but not much else.

Be aware that the way most listing agreements are written is if the buyer defaults on a deposit, the seller splits it in half with the agent. In this situation you'd only be entitled to half the deposit; the agent would get the other half.

A small deposit and a liquidated damages clause can be an invitation to a weak deal. As we've seen in previous tips, the way to better the situation is to have the buyers increase the deposit. This can be done after the major contingencies have been removed. In this case, even if you have signed the liquidated damages clause, at least the deposit will be substantial. And most buyers are hesitant to put a substantial deposit even at small risk—they're more likely to complete the transaction.

What about the Arbitration Clause?

Right along with the liquidated damages clause is usually an arbitration clause. Your agent may encourage you to sign both. The usual intent of the arbitration clause is to avoid litigation. By signing it, you agree to binding arbitration should you and the buyer have a problem. Of course, these problems are most commonly over who gets the deposit when the deal falls through.

As with liquidated damages clauses, arbitration clauses are also written in many different ways and, depending on how they are constructed, can have different consequences. You should have your attorney check the clause in your document and explain its meaning to you. Our purpose here is to look at the clause from a negotiating, not a legal, perspective

Assuming both you and the buyers sign the arbitration clause, what is the likely outcome if the buyer backs out of the deal and wants the deposit back? The outcome is that the whole mess goes to arbitration where the arbiters take a look at the deal and hand out the goodies. In many cases, like Solomon, they divide up the spoils so each party gets something. Again, there's no guarantee that you'll get the deposit. And chances are that you'll have to accept what you're given.

Depending on who the arbiters are, the arbitration can be either very expensive or not expensive at all. If professional arbiters (those belonging to the Professional Society of Arbitration) are used, the costs can be significant. If, on the other hand, real estate agents are called upon to arbitrate, the costs can be fairly light. Again, check with how the arbitration clause is written.

If I were the seller who had listed the property with an agent, I probably wouldn't mind having other agents be the arbitrators. Remember, your agent gets half the deposit and agents, while still being fair, can't help but see the deal from an agent's perspective.

On the other hand, keep in mind that you can always go to arbitration. Why give up your right to sue before you even know the circumstances?

What If You Refuse to Sign the Liquidated Damages and Arbitration Clauses?

No one can force you to sign. However, I have seen many agents stridently urge their clients to put their John Henry on the line. They operate on the assumption that by signing, in the event things go very wrong, the agent's exit from the deal will be clean. They don't like the idea of your even remotely thinking about litigation, mainly because in any litigation, the agent is likely to be named along with other parties to the deal. And agents know that, even if they prevail in court, just the costs of hiring a lawyer to defend them can be phenomenally high.

But, do you want a clean exit, or do you want to keep your rights intact? It's always a good idea to check with your attorney when you're confronted by a liquidated damages clause and an arbitration clause.

Power Tip 26
Consider Demanding the
Deposit Be Made Available to
You

So far in this chapter we've spent a lot of time worrying about
whether or not you'll get the deposit in the event the buyer backs
out of the deal through no fault of your own. There is one solution
to this problem, however, that we haven't yet covered. That's to
demand that the deposit be given directly to you.

Remember, as the seller, you're entitled to the deposit. So why not
demand it as a condition of the sale? After all, the old maxim is that
possession is nine-tenths of the law. If you possess the deposit and
feel that you're entitled to it, then it's up to the buyer to force you
to give it back. It puts the shoe on the other foot!

If I were a buyer putting up a deposit, I would be very hesitant to
make an offer if I thought the deposit were going right to the seller.
I'm not alone. Most buyers make the deposit payable to the escrow
company or the agent.

> As noted before, in theory, if the buyer makes the deposit out
> to the agent, who then deposits it in his or her fiduciary
> account, you (the seller) can demand the agent turn it over to
> you—and the agent probably should!

As we've noted earlier, buyers are hesitant about giving the seller
the deposit because they worry about two things: (1) the seller might
not be inclined to return the deposit, even if the buyer were entitled
to get it back and (2) the seller might spend the deposit and not be
able to give it back. Therefore, demanding that the buyer give the
deposit to you, the seller, is a big thing.

Will I Lose Out on Deals?

If you demand that the deposit be paid to you, will you lose out on
deals?

Possibly. If someone wants to make an offer, they most likely still
will. But, you will very likely see some amazingly small deposits.

Instead of a $5000 to $10,000 deposit, you might see a $1000 deposit. The buyers may assume (with some justification) that the money they put as a deposit is gone one way or another. If the deal goes through, it will become part of the down payment. If the deal falls through, you might not return it. Hence, they make it so small that they won't miss it, too much!

> If you are concerned that the buyer may not have enough cash to complete the transaction (down payment and closing), insist as a condition of sale that the buyer present you with evidence of sufficient cash on deposit to close. That's not an unreasonable request when the down payment is small.

Can You Get Away with Insisting on a Deposit Increase Paid To You?

One way to have your cake and eat it to, so to speak, is to agree to a very small deposit paid to you. However, as noted in Tip 24, insist that as soon as the major contingencies are removed, the buyers increase the deposit paid to you by a significant amount. This forces them to make a big decision. Assuming that all the reports come out okay (or that you negotiate an agreement on how to handle problems), they must decide either to back out or to move forward with the purchase. If they move forward, they shouldn't mind increasing the deposit, except, of course, that it's made out to you.

Why Would Buyer's Object?

Again, it's the same scenario. If you insist the buyers increase a $1000 deposit to $10,000, paid to you and the deal falls through due to no fault of theirs, they are justifiably worried you still might not return the deposit.

But, you may be thinking, how could it be through no fault of theirs? After all, they've removed their major contingencies.

True, but usually the financing contingency remains in effect until the last minute. If the buyers can't get financing, they may be entitled to the deposit back.

Further, there's always the possibility of a title problem. What if you can't deliver clear title? What if an old judgment surfaces that ties up your property and you can't sell. Yes, of course, it's unlikely, but no one can guarantee that it can't happen.

The point here is that the buyers have some right to be concerned about upping a deposit that's paid directly to you.

Should You Insist?

If you're the sort who feels that a bird in the hand is worth two in the bush, then go for an increased deposit paid to you. But don't insist on a large increase. If the buyers originally put up $1000, now ask that they increase it to $2500 or perhaps at most $5000, paid to you. In this way they may feel more comfortable with the risk you're asking them to assume.

Your goal is, or should be, to complete the deal, not to run off with the buyer's deposit. Once the buyers have removed their major contingencies and if you have a solid buyer's pre-approval letter from a lender, the chances are very high that the deal will be completed. In that case it really doesn't matter who holds the deposit. If the deal goes through, the deposit is going to just be part of the down payment anyway. So why not assuage the buyer's concern and let it go into escrow?

Should I Worry about the Deposit?

The deposit is a source of great concern on the part of both sellers and buyers. Yes, it is a necessary part of any real estate sale because it gives evidence of the buyer's sincerity when making an offer. But, in today's market, it's in no way as important a consideration as it was in the past.

Years ago (actually only a decade or two), when there were no inspection reports and no disclosures and no preapproval letters from lenders, deposits were a far more important part of the transaction. Sellers really didn't know whom they were dealing with. And buyers really didn't know much about the property they were buying.

Today, however, the preapproval letter lets the seller know well in advance of closing that the buyer can get financing. And the various disclosures and inspections lets the buyers know well in advance of closing the presumably true condition of the property. Hence, there should be far fewer suspicions and far more made deals or at least deals in which there are far fewer surprises.

Quite simply, while still important, the deposit is less important than it once was. My advice is to not go overboard in worrying about it. Pay attention to the donut and not the hole. Spend your time and efforts doing what it takes to close the deal.

7

Negotiate a Higher Price

Power Tip 27
Always Consider the Whole Offer

Probably the biggest mistake that most sellers make when consider-ing a buyer's offer is to skip immediately to the price. You're asking $200,000 and you see that the buyer is offering $185,000. What's your immediate gut reaction?

If you're like most people, it's "This is no good. The buyer isn't offering enough. I'm going to reject this offer."

That's a mistake. Yes, you may, indeed, want to reject the offer, eventually. But, hidden in all that jumble of words that makes up the offer may be jewels that would make you consider accepting less than full- price. You don't want to reject any offer out-of-hand. It's important to consider it fully.

> A deal always consists of two elements, only one of which is the price. The other, and sometimes more important, element is the terms.

Price *and* Terms

What kind of terms would make you consider a less than full-price offer? That depends on what you want out of the deal. Here's a list of some terms that you might (or might not) find appealing:.

Good Terms a Buyer Might Offer

- Higher-than-market-interest second (or first) mortgage in your favor
- The buyer will pay for all or part of your closing costs.
- Taking a problem house "as is" (not asking you to fix the problem).
- Quick close (short escrow).
- All-cash deal (when others are asking you to accept "paper").
- Letting you rent back the house for a time (if you're having trou-ble finding a place to move to).

As you can see, whether the terms are good or not depends large-ly on your own situation and the condition of the property. If you find one or more of them particularly appealing, you might indeed want to consider them in lieu of a higher price.

How to Read an Offer

Whenever you get an offer, it pays to be methodical about it. In order to understand it fully, including all of its implications, you will want to check each of the following parts, most of which will be in all offers.

> Be wary of helpers who want to interpret offers for you. The buyer's agent, who will probably present the offer, will be emphasizing its strongest points, while perhaps skimming over the weak parts. Your own agent may or may not be a strong advocate for you. Remember, none of the agents gets paid until the deal is made. An attorney can give you legal advise.

Items to Check Carefully in the Offer

1. *Is the buyer preapproved?* You want to know how qualified the buyer is to make the purchase. While you may not care about the buyer's actual name, you're looking for a strong preapproval let-ter from a lender saying that this buyer will get a mortgage suffi-ciently high to make the deal. If the buyer is putting down a substantial amount of cash, say 20 percent of the price, you also want to see a letter from a bank, certifying that the buyer has suf-ficient funds on hand to close the deal. Some smart buyers these days will even come in with a credit report to show you.

2. *How quickly can the buyer close the deal?* A buyer who's ready to close in 30 days or less indicates strength. The buyer presumably has all his or her ducks in a row in terms of financing. A buyer who needs 45 or 60 days to close may be stretching, hoping to snag financing. Or this buyer may simply be trying to tie up your property as a kind of fall back position, while looking for other, better deals. Always question why a buyer needs extra time.

3. *Are there any sweeteners?* A sweetener is a term or condition that makes the deal sweeter for you. Usually, these are the first things that agents point out. For example, you want to stay in the house an extra 2 months while your kids finish school, and the buyer is willing to go along with this. That's a sweetener.

4. *Are there any cash incentives?* Is the buyer offering to pay you extra interest on a mortgage you're willing to carry back? Is the buyer willing to pay for any of your closing costs?

5. *Is there another property involved?* Some buyers are land poor. Instead of offering a cash down payment, they may offer a mortgage on another property, or even that property itself. This complicates the deal, but could be a real boon. Be sure you have a realistic appraisal of the other property as well as a title report listing any liens so you can judge the value of the offer.

6. *Are there any negative terms?* A negative term can be anything which makes the deal less attractive to you. Contingencies which favor the buyer are negatives. Some you can expect, such as demands for a professional inspection and disclosures. Others, such as a demand that the sale be contingent on the buyer not losing his or her job or that interest rates not climb beyond a certain point, may weaken the offer. Yet others, such as a demand that the offer be contingent upon the buyer's great uncle in North Dakota coming through with a promised gift of money, may make the offer frivolous.

7. *Is the price acceptable?* Note that the price is last on this list. You won't really know if the price is acceptable until you've read the entire offer and understand it. Only then can you make a determination about whether you'll accept the price.

> Don't get hung up on price. Some foolish sellers set an arbitrary minimum price and won't budge below it. Sometimes they forgo a better deal simply because they are so determined to get that price. Be flexible. Remember that price is only one part of an overall offer.

Take Your Time

Savvy buyers will usually try to restrict the time you have for acceptance or rejection (or countering). Typically, they will make the offer good only until 12:00 midnight of the day it's presented. If you don't get the offer until 9:00 p.m., that means you only have 3 hours to accept it.

Yes, it is possible that a buyer could withdraw an offer if you don't sign by the deadline. But, if you're in the process of considering that offer, it's highly unlikely. The usual purpose of giving you a short time limit is to force you to act, not to act precipitously. Most buyers will give you enough time to make up your mind, one way or another.

What's important is not to feel pressured into making a move that doesn't feel right. You may need more time to get additional facts. You may need to consult with an attorney, or relative, or friend. Take the time to do it. It's better that you lose an offer than that you accept a bad one.

> Always take enough time to fully consider the offer.

Power Tip 28
Don't Automatically Accept
the Buyer's First Offer

Will this strategy cost you some deals? Yes, it could. But, in the long run, you should come out ahead.

First off, however, let's qualify this tip. I'm speaking of a normal to hot market. In a cold market, where prices are depressed and you haven't seen a buyer in 6 months, you may jump at the buyer's first offer. Indeed, it might be the only offer you'll get and you'd be crazy to refuse it.

However, in a more normal market and certainly in a hot market, as a general rule, you may be wiser to reject the buyer's first offer. Of course, as we shall see, there are always exceptions.

Why Should You Reject the First Offer?

While a buyer's first offer can, and sometimes does, represent the buyer's highest and best bid for your property, often it doesn't. To understand why, look at it from the buyer's perspective. If you're a buyer, besides buying the property, you've got at least three goals in making your offer:

Buyer's Goals in Making an Offer

1. To get the property for the lowest possible price.
2. To get the best possible terms.
3. To "feel out" the seller to see how "motivated" he or she is.

All of these goals speak toward making a low initial offer. It comes down to this: why offer $200,000 when the seller just might accept $180,000? Instead, offer the lower amount, first. If the seller doesn't accept it, you can always come back with a higher level offer.

When the Market's Super Hot

The exception to this strategy occurs when the market is super hot. In some areas of the country and at different times, such a high demand for property and such a shortage of inventory, that offers come in as soon as the property is listed (sometimes before the listing gets published!), and often there are multiple offers. In this situation, desperate buyers often do make their highest and best offer first.

However, in this situation, if you don't like that offer, if it's not for full price (or over full price), not accepting it shouldn't hurt. After all, someone else is likely standing in line to offer more!

Will the Buyer Offer More?

In a normal market, the answer is, "maybe." If the buyers have indeed low-balled you on the first offer, then indeed they will likely offer more. Even if the buyers offered what they considered their best, they might stretch and still offer more if they really want to buy your house.

> The market is fluid and stands still for no one. You can never know what a buyer's thinking, or what other properties a buyer is considering.

On the other hand, in the time since the first offer was made, the buyers may have reconsidered. They may have decided that they really don't want to plunge into another house. Maybe they'll continue on with the house they have. Perhaps they'll rent for a time. Or just maybe they've seen another house that they like better than yours and are no longer interested in making further offers.

This is what you risk when you reject any offer—that you won't get another offer from this buyer, that you won't even get this buyer to come back and honor the original offer, that you'll lose out on a deal that might have been made.

Even so, as a tactic for getting the most for your house, in all but a cold market and unless the offer is exactly what you want, I suggest seriously considering rejecting that first offer. Yes, you might lose a potential deal. On the other hand, you might get an even better deal.

Counter If You Don't Accept

If you don't accept the buyer's offer exactly as presented within the time frame it is offered, you've rejected it. Now it's time to make a counteroffer.

> You can't both accept and counter. The moment you make a counteroffer for a different price or terms, it's a whole new ball game. The buyer is under no obligation to accept your counteroffer and can now accept or reject it at will.

You should *always* counter any offer that you reject, no matter how frivolous the original offer may seem. I've been in a situation (in a normal market) where a would-be buyer came in with an offer that was 30 percent less than I was asking. The house was listed at $160,000 and the offer was for $112,000.

Now, that's an affront. It's just plain insulting to be offered so much less than the asking price, particularly since the house didn't have any particular problems with it that could have knocked down the price. My gut reaction was to tell this would-be buyer to take a great flying leap and simply forget about him.

However, this is business and you never know what a buyer is thinking. So I countered back, at $5000 below the asking price, indicating that I was firm and would not budge. You know what? The buyer accepted! He had simply been low-balling me to see if I was a desperate seller. When he saw I wasn't, he hunkered down and decided to pay the price.

The point here is that even if you think the buyer is insulting you, even if you think the buyer is a fool, even if you can't stand to think about this ridiculous buyer, always counter. You might lose an otherwise makable deal if you don't.

> Once you've decided to reject a would-be buyer's offer, it doesn't cost you anything to counter. You can counter for close to your asking price, your actual asking price, or even for more than you're asking! (We'll have more to say on how to counter in the next tip.) What's important is that you not be the one to close the negotiations off. Keep them open by countering.

When Should You Accept the First Offer?

There are times when you should accept the first offer, and it doesn't always have to do with market conditions. You may be desperate to sell. It could be a matter of a financial crisis (you've lost your job and can't make the payments), a divorce, a transfer, or any of a dozen other problems that have cropped up. The point here is that you need to get out, now, and you can't afford to dicker. When your back is up against the wall, you may not be able to risk negotiating for a higher price. You may simply have to accept what's on the table.

Hopefully, you'll never be in this position. But if you are, recognize the situation for what it is and act accordingly.

Never gamble if you can't afford to lose. Never reject an offer you can't live without.

Power Tip 29
Counter-Offer Carefully

Negotiation is an art, not a science. It's more akin to playing poker than to adding a row of figures. The goal, when you're the seller countering a buyer's offer, is to get the highest price and best terms that you can. It's to not walk away and leave any money lying on the table.

> Good poker players not only play the cards, they also play the other players. Good real estate sellers do the same thing.

Toward that end, once you reject the seller's initial offer, you must decide how much to counter. (As noted in the last power tip *always* counter any offer you reject.) If the market's super hot and there are buyers coming out of the woodwork, that answer could be easy: you'll counter at full price, cash. (Or more than full price, if the market's really gone berserk!)

On the other hand, if the market's more normal, you probably realize that you're not going to get your full asking price. (Indeed, you may have set your asking price higher just to leave you some wiggle room.) The question now becomes, how much lower than your asking price should you counter-offer?

Beware of Setting a Minimum Price and Countering at It

A big mistake that sellers make is to decide on a firm minimum price and then counter at it. For example, you investigate the market, you see comparables, and you eventually price your house at $340,000. But, you decide that you are really willing to accept $325,000. That's your minimum. If someone offers that, it's a deal. If someone offers less, you'll refuse to sell.

The moment you set a minimum, you box yourself in. You limit your financial flexibility. And you do yourself no good in negotiations. Here's why:

Let's say a buyer comes in at $300,000. You reject the offer; now what are you going to counter at? Your minimum is $325,000—do you counter at that?

If you do and the buyer counters back at $310,000 where do you go now? You've already given the buyer your best, lowest offer. You've got nothing left to counter back with, unless it's to repeat your previous counteroffer.

On the other hand, what if you counter at $325,000 and the buyer accepts? A good deal you say. But what if the buyer is actually willing to pay much more, say $335,000? You've lost $10,000 by countering too low.

Setting minimums doesn't do you any good. It only boxes you in and often results in your losing money on the deal, or the deal itself.

> The only time you should set a minimum is when you don't have any wiggle room. If you know you'll be lucky to get out with just paying off the mortgage, commission, and closing costs, it's reasonable to set that as your minimum price. However, even here, if someone offers just a little bit less, you might want to consider that lower offer, even if it costs cash out of your pocket, just to save your credit. Nevertheless, if you must set a minimum, don't set it in stone.

Try to Get a Sense of the Buyer

Think of your counteroffer as not the final offer in the transaction, but rather a step along the way. You counter. Then perhaps the buyer will counter your offer. And you'll counter back and on and on it can go until a price and terms are finally agreed upon, or not.

For this reason, your first counteroffer should usually not be your best and lowest. Rather, just as a buyer's first offer is often a low-ball offer, to see how you'll take it. A seller's first counter should usually be a high-ball offer to see how the buyer will take it.

If you're asking $340,000 and the buyer offers $300,000, you're $40,000 apart. You might consider countering at $335,000. This indicates to the buyer that you're willing to negotiate some. But, it also suggests that you think you've got a pretty good price and you're not really willing to drop it a whole lot. As we saw in the example in the previous tip, when I did this in an actual negotiation, the buyer caved and accepted my offer. As soon as the buyer saw I was not motivated to let my property be "stolen," he came in at close to full price.

Will all buyers respond this way? Unfortunately, no. Some will simply walk away, and you'll lose the deal.

There are buyers who simply make a lot of low-ball offers figuring that eventually they'll find a desperate seller who will accept. If you don't accept their low-ball offer, they simply move on to another property. Don't worry about losing this deal; it was never there to be made at a good price for you.

Others will counter your counter by offering close to what they originally offered, in this case say $305,000 (now you're still $30,000 apart). And, there will be some who will, indeed, simply accept your counteroffer.

Remember, any time you reject the buyers original offer and make a counteroffer, you stand to lose the deal. You're asking to open negotiations. But the buyer has the option of simply saying, "not interested," and walking away. The question is, is it a risk that's worth taking?

What If You're Close Together in Price?

Sometimes, after a few counters, you may find that you're only a few thousand dollars apart. For example, perhaps you countered at $335,000 and the buyer countered back at $330,000. Now you're only $5000 apart. Should you accept the buyer's counter?

You can. Or you can make an informal offer. You can tell the buyer's agent (or the buyer if he or she is dealing directly), "Why don't we split the difference?" If the buyer or his or her agent says, "Okay, put it in writing," you've got a deal. You've just sold your property for $332,500.

Splitting the difference can be an effective way of closing out negotiations so that everyone feels he or she got a good deal.

On the other hand, you might hold out for $335,000 and get it, or not. You never know.

What If You're Far Apart?

It's much harder if buyer and seller are far apart. You counter at $335,000 and the buyer counters at $305,000. You're $30,000 apart. That's serious money. While it's possible you could split the difference, it's unlikely.

My feeling is that in this situation I would do one of two things. I would either hold at $335,000 and convey to the buyer that this was my final offer, knowing full well that I might lose a possible deal, but hoping the buyer would come up a lot. Or, if I were highly motivated to sell, I would make a steep decline in price, perhaps to $320,000 in order to get negotiations rolling, conveying to the buyer that this was my last, best offer (which it might or might not be).

Doing this would certainly spark the buyer's interest and might get him or her to accept, or at least to make a higher counteroffer.

Is There a Time to Walk Away?

There are only two reasons to walk away from negotiations. The first is that you are truly fed up and will not budge another inch and see no way to make the deal.

The second is for effect. You really are willing to give some more, but you want the buyer to think you've made your last, best offer. You so you simply say, "Take my last offer or leave it. I'll give you an hour to decide, otherwise I'm out of here."

As a tactic, walking away can get negotiations started again, and sometimes can get your price. Or, it can cost you the deal.

There are no guarantees when negotiating real estate. The final outcome is often determined by the following percentages:

10%—how good a poker player you are.

45%—how motivated you are to sell.

45%—how motivated the buyer is to purchase.

100%—luck.

Power Tip 30
Restrict Buyers'
Contingencies

Most offers to buy in real estate are going to contain contingencies that favor the buyer. As a seller, you are going to have to accept this fact. However, you can restrict these contingencies in ways that favor and protect you.

What Is a Contingency?

A *contingency* is a clause in a purchase offer that makes the offer subject to the performance or approval of some task or event. (That's why these are also sometimes called, "Subject to" clauses.) They are typically written in the following manner, "This offer is contingent upon..." and thereafter follows the subject of the contingency.

The subject can literally be anything from the serious to the frivolous. A typical serious contingency clause makes the deal subject to the buyer obtaining financing. If the buyer doesn't get a loan, there's no deal. A frivolous contingency might make the offer subject to the buyer getting approval for the deal from her mother in another state.

Each time the buyer adds a contingency to the offer, it weakens that offer because it gives the buyer another way out, without penalty (losing the deposit). Savvy buyers add lots of contingencies because it gives them more outs, should they choose to use them.

What Are Typical Contingencies?

Most offers will include several of the following contingencies:

- *Financing contingency.* The buyer doesn't get a loan, there's no deal.
- *Disclosure contingency.* The buyer has the right to approve your disclosures. No approval; no deal.
- *Professional inspection.* The buyer has the right to approve an inspection report. No approval; no deal.
- *Title approval.* The buyer has the right to clear title. You can't supply one; no deal.

- *Termite clearance.* You can't supply termite clearance, no deal.
- *Other reports. (geological, flood, and so on):* Buyer doesn't approve; no deal.
- *Bond payoff.* You pay off existing public bonds on the property. You don't pay; no deal.

As you can see, all of these contingencies favor the buyer. If you don't perform as the buyer demands, he or she can simply walk away from the deal with clean hands. Or, depending on how it was written, take you to court to force you to pay perform as you agreed.

What Can You Do about Contingencies?

Your First Line of Defense Is to Strip Them Away.
You can counter the buyer's offer by eliminating the contingencies in a counteroffer. Simply cross them out. The buyer either purchases your house without contingencies, or there's no deal.

> Your agent will explain the actual method preferred in your area for rejecting contingencies. But remember, even if you don't change the price, the moment you change the sales agreement, for example, by removing a contingency, you've rejected the buyer's off and you're countering. The buyer may or may not accept.

In all but the very hottest market, however, there's usually going to be "no deal." Most buyers realize that most of these contingencies are necessary to protect them. They feel they must have the financing contingency, in case their loan doesn't go through. They must have the right to approve an inspection report, in case your property happens to have a sink hole underneath. And so on.

So as a practical matter, it's unlikely you'll be able to simply remove most buyer's serious contingencies and still have a deal.

Your Second Line of Defense Is to Restrict the Contingencies.
Restricting contingencies makes it harder for the buyer to use them

as an excuse to back out of the deal. By restricting a buyer's contingencies, you sweeten the offer to favor you.

How Do I Restrict the Contingencies?

There are at least three ways you can restrict a contingency: time, money, and performance:

Restricting the Time on a Contingency A buyer is very likely to demand the right to approve a professional inspection report. You're simply going to have to concede this to get the deal.

> The inspection report actually protects you, the seller. After having an inspection done, a buyer is much less likely to come back later on and say there was a hidden problem with the property. See Chapter 8.

However, you don't have to let the buyer dawdle on about the inspection report indefinitely. You can limit the time for the buyer's approval. A typical restriction is 2 weeks. Yes, the buyer can have the property professionally inspected. But, if the inspection isn't completed and the buyer's approval given within 14 days, there's no deal. You're not obligated to proceed and may begin selling the house to someone else. (Or alternatively, depending on how it's written, if the buyer doesn't disapprove within two weeks, the assumption is that the property is okay and the deal moves forward.)

This puts the onus on the buyer. He or she must move quickly to get that report and either approve or disapprove it. Yes, the buyer can still back out, but only during the next 14 days. After that, the buyer must bite the bullet and approve the report (or negotiate with you over any problems) or back out. No dawdling.

The same holds true for the disclosures and any other reports the buyer may want.

You can add a contingency of your own, here, namely, that you have the right to continue showing the property and accept back-up offers until the buyer removes a contingency. This puts additional pressure on the buyer to act.

Restricting the Money on a Contingency You may also restrict the contingency in terms of money. For example, the buyer demands that you put a fence around the yard as a condition of sale (subject to). You have to agree that the yard needs a fence, particularly since you've got a pool and that poses a health and safety hazard. So you agree to the fence. But, you limit the amount of money you'll spend on it. For example, you'll put up a fence, provided it doesn't cost more than $2000.

Or, you agree to provide a termite clearance, which means having an inspection and paying for repair of damage, provided it doesn't cost more than $2500. Restricting the money amount leaves you a way out. If it turns out it will cost more, there's no deal. Or you can reopen negotiations

Restricting the amount of money you'll pay for a termite clearance usually sends up a red flag to the buyer. "Why is the seller worried about termites?" the buyer is likely to ask. Adding this restriction could cause a wary buyer to back out of the deal by refusing to sign your counter. Be careful with what and how you restrict contingencies.

Restricting the Performance of a Contingency You can also restrict how the buyer must perform on a contingency. For example, a typical financing contingency will say something such as the purchase is subject to the buyer obtaining a 30-year fixed-rate loan for not more than 8.5 percent interest. (Usually, the interest rate is mentioned because it determines the monthly payment, and most buyers have a maximum monthly payment for which they can qualify.)

However, you realize that it will take 30 days to close the deal and interest rates, currently at 8.5 percent, are rising sharply. What if at the end of 30 days, when the deal is ready to close, interest rates have moved up to 8.75 percent? Suddenly, the buyer doesn't have to close and can simply walk away from the deal.

One way of restricting this is to counter the interest rate. Instead of the 8.75 percent current rate, you change it to 9.5 percent. The buyer must move forward if the market interest rate moves as high as 9.5 percent.

But, what if the buyer can't qualify at 9.5 percent? You've got a weak buyer who may not be able to complete the purchase in any event. Besides, you're not really asking for something unreasonable. If the buyer can't get the mortgage for any reason, the overall financing contingency applies and he or she can still walk away. By raising the interest-rate restriction, you've just made sure the buyer doesn't have an easy out.

Who Writes in the Restriction?

Typically, real estate agents or attorneys will write up the original offer, including any contingencies. Therefore, you should have a knowledgeable agent or attorney write up your restriction. The language is important and if it's done improperly, it could have unanticipated consequences. If you're not a savvy seller in this area, have a competent person do it for you.

Power Tip 31
Discover the Buyer's
Motivation

The *Buyer's motivation* is the reason he or she has for wanting to buy your house. *"Seller's motivation"* is the more commonly used phrase, and it refers to the buyer divining how eager you are to sell and using that information to get a better deal. You can play the same game. It usually begins at the time the buyer makes an offer.

How Can I Use Motivation
Knowledge?

There are many ways, and all affect whether and how good a deal you can get.

Ways to Use Knowledge of the Buyer's Motivation

- You learn that the buyers are torn between two properties and are not really sure which they want to buy. They've made an offer on yours which can only be described as tentative. You want to use kid gloves with these buyers. They may fade away at the slightest resistance on your part. Like hooking a fish that's given a tenuous nibble, you have to very carefully draw in your line. If you really want to sell, you'll concede price, terms, and contingencies.

- On the other hand, you learn that the buyers have simply fallen in love with your house. It's perfect for their kids, who love the back yard. It's close to school, to work, it's the right size and price. They'll simply do anything to get it. Okay, now you're in the driver's seat. You can feel relatively secure in countering their offer for more money and better terms. You can strip away contingencies. In short, with devoted buyers, you can almost write your own deal. ("Almost" because you can always go too far and force any buyer away.)

- You learn that the buyers like your house, but it's at the upper end of their financing capabilities. They're putting in all the cash they have and if the monthly payment goes up another $25, they just won't be able to qualify and the deal will fall through. With this kind of buyer, you can work other angles of the deal. It's unlikely you'll be able to get a better price out of them; they might be willing, but simply can't afford it. On the other hand, they might make concessions on timing—when you need to get out. They may be willing to let you live in the house an extra 3 months rent-free. Or perhaps they'll overlook an old roof that needs replacing. Or they may simply not demand that you fix all sorts of items that are broken. All of these concessions on their part can add up to a significant savings on your part. And you can demand them because you understand their motivation.

- Or, finally, the buyers love your house, but are trying to steal it. You learn that they have plenty of cash in the bank and can afford twice the estimated monthly payment your house will cost them. Yes, they like your house, but they are making a low-ball offer, hoping to get a great deal. Of course, now that you know their motivation for the low-ball offer, you don't let them get away with it. You come back with a high counter and get a much better deal.

Knowing *why* the buyers are making the offer that they are making is as important as understanding the offer itself.

> The old maxim is that "cash is king;" however, in most deals the real king is knowledge.

How Do I Discover the Buyer's Motivation?

That, of course, is the rub. Just as sellers don't like to reveal just how eager they are to sell for fear of getting low-balled, buyers don't like to reveal their true motivation for fear of getting high-balled.

Nevertheless, there are ways to discover just what your buyers are thinking.

Discovering What Your Buyer's Are Thinking

- *Ask them.* Chances are that you, your spouse, or someone from your side will be around when the buyers tour the house. If they seem interested, ask them if the house would fill their needs? Will it be suitable for their children? What about work, is it close by? What about size and neighborhood—is it what they are looking for? Do they like two stories or one? And so on. It's positively amazing what buyers will tell you, once you establish rapport.

> Serious buyers usually come by to see a house more than once. If you learn that a buyer is coming by a second time, try to be around. It's a great opportunity to ask questions. Only don't be too much of a busybody—you might scare the buyers away!

- *Ask your agent to ask the buyers' agent.* (Or ask their agent yourself.) Agents want to make deals. After all, it's the only way they get paid. Hence, even though they shouldn't, they may be very talkative about how enthusiastic (or unenthusiastic) the buyers are.

- *Analyze the offer.* Sometimes you can read between the lines. For example, if the buyers are adamant that the children's play equipment in the yard be included as part of the sale (normally you would take it with you), it suggests that the house may be perfect for their kids. Of if they insist you leave the workbench and some of the power tools in the garage, perhaps one of the buyers is in love with your work area. Or if they insist you leave the refrigerator because it matches the colors of the kitchen, perhaps it speaks to their really liking that area of your house. No, this is not a science. But sometimes you can learn volumes from what extras the buyers want.

- *Analyze their counteroffer.* I was once in extended negotiations with a buyer, trying to get her to increase her price. She was coming back with higher offers, but still not matching my demands. Then, on what I subsequently learned was her last offer, she moved up only a couple of thousand dollars, but suddenly insisted that I throw in the washer and dryer and some cabinets (which I had intended leaving anyhow, but which at this point hadn't been mentioned in the deal). My analysis was that this buyer had reached her last straw. This was evidenced by the fact that she only came up a little, but more importantly, that she demanded some personal property as a way of compensating for the increased price. My thinking was that either I could accept this offer, or I would lose the deal. I accepted it, and the deal was made.

While you can never know for sure that the buyers are thinking, you can often come close. It's how you use that knowledge that can make a better deal for you

Never push a buyer who's wavering on the fence. You might just cause them to fall the other way and forget about buying your house. On the other hand, always push a buyer who's in love with your property. You'll be astounded at how much they are willing to concede.

Power Tip 32
Be Willing to Give on Price to
Get Better Terms

This is often the difference between getting a better deal, or no deal at all. In any real estate transaction there are always two elements. One element is price. The other is terms. Think of these as two people sitting on a seesaw. As one goes down, the other goes up and vice versa. It's rare, but not impossible, to get both better price and better terms. More often, they are a trade-off, one for the other.

The reason that this trade-off is so important is that often buyers (and many times sellers, too) are hung up on price. It becomes a matter of ego. The buyers feel that they shouldn't pay more than a certain, specific amount for your house. Perhaps they've heard that houses in the area go for a certain price, and they don't want to pay more than that price. Or maybe they feel that they simply don't want to extend themselves beyond a certain arbitrary point.

> Buyers often set limitations on their finances that don't exist in the real world. They may say that they don't want to pay more than $2000 a month in payments (to go higher on the loan and price), even though lenders say they can comfortably afford to pay $3000. If the buyers are adamant about this, then it's probably better to try to negotiate a different area of the deal.

Or maybe the buyers simply are looking to get a "steal" and are unwilling to pay a realistic price.

Whenever you come up against the hard wall of price resistance, recognize it for what it is. Regardless of the cause behind it, it usually means that you're not going to get the buyers to come up with a much higher price. It's at that point that a savvy seller begins to negotiate terms.

What Terms Can I Negotiate?

The sky is limit. Here are a few that you might find give you a better deal:

Terms That Might Give the Seller a Better Deal

- *A higher interest rate.* If you're carrying back a first or second mortgage as part of the deal and the buyers refuse to budge on price, demand a higher interest rate. If the market rate is, for example, 8 percent, demand 10 percent. On a $100,000 mortgage, that's around $2000 a year or roughly $10,000 over 5 years. You might be willing to concede that much in price to gain that much on the interest.

- *Closing costs.* Have the buyers pay part or all of your closing costs. Buyers often demand that sellers pay their closing costs; there's no reason you can't turn the tables. Give the buyers their price, but have them pay for your share of title insurance and escrow charges, which can often be as much as $5000 or more, depending on the size of the deal. You could even demand they pay your pro-rations (your payback to them for interest, taxes, and other charges they will pay in advance) or commission, although buyers are much more reluctant to take these charges upon themselves.

- *Repairs.* If there are major repairs, such as to the roof, the heating/cooling system, and so on and the buyers refuse to budge on price, demand that they accept the property as is. This could save you the cost of the repairs, which could amount to a great many thousands of dollars.

- *Timing.* Maybe you want to stay longer because the kids are in school for another 3 months. The buyers won't budge on price, so you demand that they allow you to stay on the property rent-free for that period of time. That could be worth several thousand dollars a month, depending on your living expenses. Or, perhaps you need to get out very quickly, within 2 weeks because of a job move or another house you're buying or whatever. Yes, you'll concede on price, provided the buyers concede timing to you.

- *Personal property.* You were planning on throwing in the SubArtic refrigerator (a $3500 value), the furniture (a $15,000 value), and other personal items. But, you can use these in your next house. So while giving on price, you take these with you.

These are just a few of the terms you might want to trade off for a concession on price.

Every deal is different, with different terms and price problems. What you're willing to trade for price could be anything. Try to be creative.

How Do I Offer Terms for Price?

It's all part of the negotiations. The buyers make an offer, you counter, they counter, and after a while, it becomes very clear that they simply aren't going to budge on price.

Now you make a counter on terms. Here, you accept the buyers' last price offer and instead counter on terms. You might be shocked at what buyers are willing to trade away in order to get that stiff price that they are demanding. In fact, sometimes it would appear that buyers are irrational, trading away terms that are worth far more than that the higher price you were previously asking!

If you're going to counter on terms, it's usually a good idea to accept the buyer's last offer on price. This way it makes it perfectly clear to the buyers that they will get their price. If you counter even a little bit higher on price, as well as terms, you can turn the buyers off. Once you've determined the buyers' highest price, don't argue over it—try to get concessions on the terms.

Going the Other Way

As long as we're talking about trade-offs, be sure you don't overlook trading terms for price. You might find a buyer who's hung up on terms. In that case, you can negotiate a higher price!

For example, a friend was once selling a house with a very fancy crystal chandelier hanging in the entranceway. The chandelier was created by an Italian artist and was worth close to $10,000. The sellers indicated that they were taking it with them. In fact, they had a sign hanging right on the chandelier which said, "sellers' personal property—does not go with the sale."

Of course, the first offer they got included the chandelier as part of the sale. The buyers included a contingency which made the chandelier part of the real estate.

The sellers countered on price and, of course, deleted the chandelier contingency. They were definitely taking it with them; they felt that the buyers had simply asked for it on the odd chance they might get it.

Wrong! The buyers loved the chandelier. Indeed, their agent said they simply would not purchase the house if the chandelier was not included.

The sellers now had a decision to make. Should they give up the chandelier? They could always get another for $10,000. So they bumped the price up $12,000, and agreed to throw in the chandelier. The buyers accepted!

You never know what buyers will accept until you offer. And sometimes when a buyer is hung up on a term, you can get a major concession in price.

You should always remove any personal property you have prior to showing your house for sale. If the sellers wanted to keep the expensive chandelier, they should have removed it and replaced it with a less expensive one. What buyers don't see, they can't ask for.

Power Tip 33
Don't Give the Buyers Long
to Accept Your Counter-
Offer

Timing is the essence of many things from comedy to football. It is also very important in real estate, particularly in making deals.

If you've received offers from buyers, (as noted earlier) you'll quickly notice that many of them (the good ones) give you only a short time to make up your mind. You might find that you get an offer presented at 6:00 p.m. in the evening and you only have until 12:00 midnight to accept.

Why the pressure, you may have asked yourself? Are the buyers so anxious to purchase? Or do they have other properties they want to make offers on? Why are they only giving me a few hours?

The answer is threefold: First, they want you to make a decision right away. If you have lots of time to think about it, you might talk yourself into, and then out of, their offer. Second, they don't want someone else to slip in with a better offer. If they give you time, another buyer might come by. And third, they don't want to be committed to you for longer than necessary. They, indeed, want to keep their options open looking for other properties.

When you counter their offer, the same rules apply.

Why You Want to Give Buyers a Short Time Frame

1. You want the buyers to act immediately on your counteroffer. Give them 3 days to think it over, and you're more likely to produce a stalemate. Give them 3 hours, and they are likely to act one way or another (to accept, reject, or counter your counter.)

> Buyers, like sellers and everyone else, tend to procrastinate. If they've got 3 hours to make a decision, it will take that long. If they have 3 days, time will expand to take that long.

2. If you give the buyers a long time, to think about your offer, they could also be out there looking at other property. And they just

might discover a house that they like better than yours. Remember, when you counter, you've rejected their original offer. They are off the hook. They can simply walk away from your counteroffer without a comment.

3. Finally, you might get a better offer. As long as your counter is out there, you're committed to the buyers. True, you can cancel it at any time. But, what if you get another, better offer and just as you decide to cancel your counteroffer to the first buyers, they accept? Can't you hear all the shouting, name-calling, and confusion that would ensue? Better to give the buyers a short time to accept.

How Do You Give a Short Time Frame?

On the form for every counter-offer (and offer) is a line to be filled in that states for how long the offer is good. Is it good until 12:00 midnight, today's date? Until 12:00 noon the following day? Or what?

How you fill in that line determines for how long the offer remains in force. Once that deadline is passed, the offer becomes null and void, a dead thing.

By filling in a time, you set a deadline. You give the buyers until then to act.

What If My Agent Cautions against a Short Deadline?

Be sure to ask why. Your agent might have a very good reason, although I can't think of one.

Most agents who caution against short deadlines are simply timid. They don't like thrusting a strict demand from the sellers onto the buyers. Some feel it's simply impolite. Others think that it's too pushy. Yet others think it limits their flexibility.

None of these is the case. A short deadline actually empowers your agent. It allows him or her to say to the seller, "You have to act now, or else my seller's offer will expire and you'll lose the house." It gives the agent the flexibility to secure a counter, if the buyers won't accept.

Maybe it is pushy, but then again, that's part of getting a good deal signed.

Don't accept that the agent can't reach the buyers. Buyers who make offers make themselves available. They want to know what your reaction was. Did you accept? Did you counter? Besides, with cell- phones, faxes, e-mails, and Federal Express, there's virtually no one on the planet who can't be reached in a matter of a few minutes or hours.

What If They Don't Act before the Deadline?

The other side of the coin is that the buyers simply may not act before the deadline. They may have trouble deciding among themselves what to do. Or they may need new information; for example, will the lender give them a higher mortgage which will, in turn, allow them to offer more on your property?

If your agent reports that the buyers can't come to a decision and need more time for reasons such as those just given, you may want to give them more time. There's no reason you can't extend your deadline, if it suits your purpose.

Just be sure that when you extend your deadline, you set a new one. If the buyers are arguing among themselves and it's late at night, agree to give them another 18 hours. Perhaps they'll see things more clearly in the morning. If, however, they are still arguing among themselves, then maybe there isn't a deal to be made, here. Sometimes, when buyers argue, it really means they aren't sure they want to buy anything at all. You may simply want to back away and look for other buyers.

If you give them more time to get lender approval, or to come up with more cash, or to have a trusted financial advisor look over the deal, again set a reasonable deadline based on how long it will take for them to satisfy their needs. Just remember, however, the longer you give them, in general, the less favorable it is for you.

What If They Walk Away?

It could happen. The buyers simply walk away from the deal. They say no to your counteroffer and don't counter themselves. They simply are no longer interested. It's happened to me and to every other seller who's been in the business long enough.

Don't worry about it. Some deals just weren't born to be completed. Maybe the buyers were just trying to steal the property with a low-ball offer. Maybe they found another house that turns them on more. Maybe they decided not to buy. Maybe any of a hundred different things could happen. However, by setting a deadline, you gave it your best shot. Some deals simply can't be made.

Some buyers will make one low-ball offer after another on different properties, hoping to catch a desperate seller. They never accept any counteroffers!

Power Tip 34
Counter for More Than Your
Asking Price

Counter for more than you're asking for the property? Impossible?

It all depends on the market. In a cold or even a normal market, it certainly would be impossible. But in the overheated markets we've had at various times and places in the country, it's not impossible, not even unlikely.

When there are buyers coming out of the woodwork and no houses for sale, then a counter for more than you're asking might, indeed, be in order. First, let's be clear on what's meant here.

You're asking $200,000 for your house. A buyer comes in offering $190,000. Instead of countering at $195,000 or even $200,000, you instead counter at $210,000. Why would you do that? Why would a buyer accept?

Unusual Markets

Let's look at if from a the buyers' perspective. They've been trying to buy a house for months. They've gone out with a dozen agents. They've made offers on houses, always coming in a day later or a dollar short.

Now, they find your house. They like the place and decide to make an offer. It's only been 3 days since it's been listed. Yet, while they were looking at the property, they saw a dozen other potential buyers looking as well. Some of them even seemed to be in the process of writing up an offer.

So, they've made you an offer. Now, you come back with a serious counteroffer. You're offering to sell them the property for *more* than the asking price. If they simply laugh and walk away, they know that, given the market conditions, someone else will be right there to take their place. And very likely will offer more than the asking price. So, do they accept your counter? Maybe!

> When the market is irrationally hot, irrational counteroffers do get accepted. In fact, in such a market you may simply not be getting enough for your house if you just accept full price!

How Much Is the House Really Worth?

When the market's stable, that is, it's not going up or down much, that's easy to determine. You simply get a list of comparable sales for the past 6 months (as described in Tip 2), add or subtract for differences, and that, for sure, is the price. You can bank on it.

However, when the market is rising (or falling), it's a different story. It becomes much harder to get a handle on what the correct price might be. Comparables tend to show what the price was, a few months ago, not what it is today.

When the market's going up, one way of dealing with this is to add a certain percentage for price inflation. For example, if the market's rising 6 percent a year, then find out what the comps of 6 months ago sold for and add 3 percent (for half a year's price inflation). That should be pretty close to current valuations. Close, but not necessarily on the money. By now, the market might have slowed down or might be spurting higher.

Thus, in a rising (or falling) housing market, all you can do is guesstimate what the correct asking price is. You'll quickly find out how close you are by how buyers react. If they stay away, you know you're asking too much. On the other hand, if they bombard you with offers, then the chances are you're asking too little.

There's no reason you can't counter for more than you're asking. The asking price is a goal that you're aiming toward. You can easily shoot right past your goal and get even more.

Will Buyers Pay More?

You won't know until you ask. However, if you misjudge the market, you could end up with egg on your face. Your buyer may simply depart from the scene, thinking that you're loony. And you may find that other buyers don't materialize. Before demanding more than your asking price, be sure of the following:

What to Check Out before Demanding More Than the Asking Price

- *Is the overall market hot?* Real estate agents can easily provide you with this information. Local papers also will be running stories about the overheated market. If you learn that your market area is not hot, don't ask more than your asking price. But do try to negotiate your way up to as close to it as possible.

- *Do you have more than one buyer?* Just because the market's hot doesn't mean that buyer's are necessarily interested in your property. You can tell if they are, however, because of multiple offers. If after only a few days on the market, your house is drawing many offers from at least two or more buyers, chances are your house is hot. Now, it's time to consider demanding more than your asking price.

- *Are buyer's coming back with counters?* If you counter at more than your asking price and you never see the buyer again, reconsider doing it for the next buyer. Reevaluate your situation. Could it be that the market has cooled down a bit since you last looked at it? Could it be that your house isn't in quite the demand you thought it was? You don't want to demand more than any buyer is willing to pay.

- *What do the agents say?* Agents always seem to be behind the market. That's only natural, since they are still closing the deals they made last month and the month before. Nevertheless, if they begin shaking their heads and saying things like, "I've never seen anything like this," it's a good sign that you're in an overheated market.

Your goal is to get the best deal that you can for yourself. That means not leaving anything on the bargaining table. Think how foolish you'll feel if you *only* get your full asking price (remarkable in itself) only to learn that buyers are paying 5 or 10 percent over asking price!

Demanding more than your asking price is assuredly a risky tactic. If you've guessed wrong about circumstances, it's likely to backfire against you. Besides, an agent could claim a commission for bringing in a buyer "ready, willing, and able" to pay the asking price.

But, when houses are "selling like hotcakes," you'll probably kick yourself if you don't at least try for more.

8

Do Yourself a Favor on Disclosures and Inspections

Power Tip 35
Disclose Everything

This is solid advice and, as far as I'm concerned, there are no exceptions to the rule. When you have to disclose any defects in the property to buyers, be rigorous, thorough, and honest. It will pay off in the long run.

Sellers, when faced with giving disclosure statements to buyers, frequently ask such things as, "Can I not mention the cracks in the concrete?" "What about the broken fence post at the far back of the yard?" "Does it matter that there are roots in the drain line, it only clogs up every 6 months or so?" "What about the roof? It's not leaking right now." "Can't I just not mention these things?" And on and on.

The temptation is to skip over those areas which are likely to cause headaches or which could even derail the deal. Many of us feel that it's better to let sleeping dogs lie than to wake them with problematic disclosures.

This, however, is one case where it pays in the long run to be as complete and detailed as possible.

What Are Disclosures?

In most states today sellers are required to give disclosures to buyers. (Even in those states where they are not required by law, most buyers demand them as a condition of the purchase.) The disclosures cover most things about the property, defects in particular. Here's what a typical disclosure list might include.

Typical Disclosure List

- Any appliances that go with the property—stove, dishwasher, clothes dryer, and so on.
- Any fixtures that go with the property—such as light fixtures, security alarms, and so on.
- Any safety features—such as smoke or CO_2 alarms, indoor fire sprinklers, earthquake or wind retrofitting, water heater tie-down, and so on.
- Any neighborhood nuisances—such as barking dogs, loud neighbors who are frequently the subject of police calls, and so on.

- Any environmental hazards—such as a nearby dump site, nearby oil tanks, earthquake or flood zone, and so on.

- Any reports that have been made on the property—such a professional inspection, termite, soil, roofing, and so on.

- Any pets that were kept on the property—such as a dog, cat, bird, and so on.

- Any defects in the structure—such as cracks in the foundation, slab, walls, ceilings, and so on

- Any defects in the house systems—such as problems with the heating, cooling, potable water, waste water, electrical, and other systems.

- Any water problems—such as standing water in the basement, runoff water during storms, roof leaks, and so on.

- Any problems with the title—such as liens or encumbrances.

- Anything else at all that affects the property—from a leaky faucet to a broken window screen.

What's important to understand is that the preceding list is only a tiny portion of what's in a good disclosure report. (To see a typical disclosure report, check into my book *The Home Inspection Trouble Shooter*, Dearborn, 1995.) A full report can have more than a hundred different entries and cover every possible element of the house.

> You are usually required to disclose every defect that you know, or should know, about the property. This means that you may want to have your own professional inspection to be sure you haven't overlooked something (such as a leaky gas line) that you should have known about, but didn't!

Why Should You Want to Give Full Disclosure?

It's easy to see why a buyer would want to get full disclosure. A buyer wants to know what he or she is buying, and disclosures help define it. The best example here is when a buyer offers to purchase a house for $350,000, subject to disclosures. However, the disclosures reveal a cracked foundation which will cost some $120,000 to fix. Is the house still worth $350,000? Or it is really only worth $230,000 (minus the cost of fixing the foundation, not to mention the hassle).

An offer is normally based on the property being in good condition. If there's something wrong with it, then the offer normally will be adjusted downward to compensate for the problem.

> Put simply, a house with a problem just isn't worth as much as a house without a problem.

That, of course, sounds like a good reason *not* to reveal defects to buyers—when revealed, the buyers will just cut their price!

Indeed, the old maxim *caveat emptor* (let the buyer beware) prevailed for nearly a century and was based on just such a premise. The seller would paint and plaster and patch to conceal all sorts of problems. And it was the buyer's headache after the sale.

However, when housing prices soared in the late 1970s and through the 1980s, too much money became at stake. Buyers were losing their life savings in shoddy properties. Hence, a series of lawsuits against sellers (and their agents) resulted in reversals of sales.

To protect buyers (and indirectly to protect sellers from buyers' reprisals), disclosures came into vogue. Sellers now tell buyers everything that they know of that's wrong with the property. And if buyers then go ahead with the purchase, knowing full well the problems, they have very little to complain about later on.

Thus, the disclosures protect both parties.

But Won't Disclosures Ruin a Sale?

Disclosure of serious defects might indeed cost a sale, although far more often it's simply a matter of negotiating over who pays to have the problem fixed. However, better to lose the sale now than to have to take the property back and pay damages later on.

Besides, disclosures have become so common these days that most buyers simply take them in stride. They assume that there's going to be a whole list of problems. And as long as there aren't any really severe ones, often the buyers don't even complain about them.

Should I Really Disclose Everything?

Yes. I disclose everything when I sell a house. I even disclose things which might be wrong, but which I'm not sure about. I even disclose things that aren't serious but which might hide serious defects.

As an example, I always reveal that there are cracks in the foundation, the slab, the floors, the walls, and the ceilings, even if these aren't visible! Why? Because such cracks are normal and by themselves mean little; however, they can hide serious structural problems which I may not know about. By disclosing all the cracks , I don't let the buyers come back later on and accuse me of hiding anything.

If it's an old roof, I always say that it could leak, although it hadn't in the last rain; that the old fence is potentially falling over, even though it looks straight; that the heating system is old and could break down although it's currently working, and so on.

> Buyers quickly get the idea when you begin disclosing everything. They have their own inspector check it out and if nothing serious turns up, they realize that you are just protecting yourself.

Of course, if there's anything obviously wrong, certainly always disclose that as well.

Disclosures won't hurt you if you do them correctly. If there is a problem, it should be fixed and it may be that you need to pay for it. It's one of the things that goes with house ownership and sale.

Remember, you really can't sell at Cadillac price if what you've got under the paint job is a Chevy.

Power Tip 36
What If the Buyer
Disapproves the Disclosures?

You dutifully fill out an extensive disclosure form that your agent gives you (or that you get from an agent or escrow company if you're selling on your own). Following the advice in Tip 35, you disclose everything that is wrong with your property. You present the disclosures to the buyers and 2 days later are informed that they have disapproved them.

What do you do now?

Find Out Why?

Usually when buyers disapprove disclosures, it comes in one of two ways. The buyers can simply say they disapprove of the disclosures and don't want to discuss it further. They get their deposit back and they disappear, never to be heard from again. Or the buyers can see it's an invitation to negotiate.

Why Buyer's Disapprove Disclosures

When Buyers Just Bug Out   When buyers simply say no and leave, you can pretty well figure that, unless you disclosed something rather terrible, they've just lost interest in the property. Many times buyers will want to tie up a house for a few days (so others can't get it) while they make up their minds. One way to do this is the disclosures. If, for example, they have 3 days to disapprove them, it gives them that length of time to consider the purchase. Then, if they decide not to buy, no matter what the disclosures say, they simply disapprove.

> Some states have a set number of days during which buyers can disapprove the disclosures from the time they receive them. In California, for example, it's 3 days. For this reason it is wise to give all potential buyers a set of disclosures as soon as possible to get the clock running. Be sure they sign for them and date the receipt.

There's really nothing you can do about this. The buyers have just decided against buying your property. Think of it like fishing. You had a big one on the line and, at the last minute, it slipped off the hook and got away. Just forget these buyers.

On the other hand, you must reconsider if you actually disclosed something really significant. For example, if your disclosures revealed that your house was sliding down a hill and that it would cost $70,000 to correct it, maybe the buyers got scared away.

If there's a really big problem, many buyers simply don't want to deal with it. They don't want to hear how it might be cured, the steps you're willing to take, or anything else. They just want to get as far away from the problem as possible.

If this is the case, then with your *next* buyers, you should be sure to get the problem out front. Be sure they understand that yours is a "problem house." That way, by the time they make an offer and you give them disclosures, you can be sure they already know they're delving into troubled waters. This way, you save yourself a lot of wasted time and effort on those buyers who would never consider the property anyhow.

When Buyers Want to Negotiate On the other hand, there are some buyers who still want to buy your property, but see either a necessity or an opportunity for negotiations. You may have disclosed something that worries them. For example, perhaps you said that the roof leaked in last winter's rain, but that you had it patched and it does not leak at this time. (You normally only need to provide a roof that does not leak—not a new roof.)

The buyers are concerned that they'll be getting an old roof that will leak again in the future. They will approve the disclosures, provided you put on a new roof, up to their specifications.

When this happens, you have to assess the buyers. Are they really worried about the roof? Or do they just want a price concession from you? Or is it both.

The fact is that even if you have patched an old roof, chances are it will leak again. Consequently, in order to sell your house in a normal to weak market, you'll probably have to do something about the roof. (In a hot market, there are so many buyers, you can afford to blow off those who complain and wait until you get buyers who will take the property "as is.")

Now you can negotiate. Okay, you say that you understand the roof is a problem. You'll credit the buyers with $5000 toward replacing it.

They say they're really worried all their furniture will get wet in the next rainstorm. How about $10,000? You continue to negotiate and eventually settle at $7000.

Yes, it has cost you money. But you have sold the house and you've made a big problem go away.

Don't Take No for an Answer

One of the big problems with buyers who disapprove disclosures is that you won't know if they are bugging out or just want a price concession, unless you ask. Sometimes the buyers or their agents will be straightforward about it. "My buyers disapprove the disclosures, but will move forward if you fix the roof," the agent may say. Now, at least you know where you stand.

On the other hand, you may simply hear nothing. If that's the case, make the call. Phone the buyer's agent, or the buyers themselves, and ask what the problem is. Sometimes it's as simple as failed communications. You may be able to save your deal, just by offering to negotiate over a problem the buyers have with your disclosures.

Don't Take the Problem Out of the Disclosures

After you've had a buyer turn down the property because of something you disclosed (or after it's happened more than once), you're going to be very tempted to remove the offending disclosure. For example, I once had an agent friend who had some sellers who indicated on their initial disclosures that their roof leaked. When a buyer refused to purchase because of that disclosure, they redid the document. The next disclosure they handed to a potential buyer said only, "Some stains on the ceiling of the top floor."

When their agent asked about the change, they pointed out that the roof leaked, but now it was summer and that the stains were the only thing visible of the leaks. (Rainwater during the winter rainy season had run down onto the ceilings staining them.) All anyone could see of the former leaks were the stains.

When the agent suggested that perhaps that was concealing the real problem, they said they didn't care—let the buyers figure it out. They only wanted to sell. The agent then disclosed that the roof leaked on her own disclosures. (In some states agents must make "agent disclosures.") The sellers were outraged. However, it all blew over when the next buyer bought the house and negotiated half the price of a new roof.

Once you create a set of disclosures, you can't remove it from existence; remember, the buyers you gave it to have it. If you give a different set of disclosures to a new set of buyers and if the first and second buyers ever get together to compare disclosures, you could be in hot water.

Power Tip 37
Insist That the Buyers Have a
Professional House
Inspection

What? Insist that the buyers inspect the house professionally, even if they don't want to? This sounds like snatching defeat from the jaws of victory! If the buyers are foolish enough not to want a house inspection, why would any seller be foolish enough to insist they have one?

The reason is that the house inspection helps protect you, the seller. Read on.

What Is a House Inspection?

A professional house inspection allows the buyers to select any professional inspector they choose to come and spend as long as necessary (within reasonable bounds) to look anywhere (without, of course, damaging the house) for defects. It gives the buyers the opportunity to check out the property to their heart's content.

Further, if the buyers aren't sure about something, it usually allows them to call in other professionals. Here's a list of possible pros that buyers could call as part of the inspection process:

Roofing inspector

Electrical inspector

Plumbing inspector

Soil engineer

Heating/air-conditioning inspector

Structural engineer

Any other professional to inspect a part of the house

Most real estate sales agreements specify that the professional inspection does *not* include inspectors from the local building and safety department. In other words, the buyers cannot call the city in to inspect the property. The reason is that if the city inspectors come in and find something wrong, they might condemn the building and close it until the problem is fixed! The buyers could disappear, and you'd have to fix the problem—not something a seller would be thrilled to have happen.

Once the buyers have satisfied themselves that there are no major defects, or if there are, that you and they will negotiate how to handle them, the buyers normally approve the inspection report. And you can proceed with the sale.

What the Buyers' Approval Means

The buyers' professional inspection report is a two-edged sword. From the buyers' perspective, it allows them to check out the property for defects. They can learn for themselves what it is they are buying. They can ensure themselves that your house is no, "pig in a poke."

However, from your (the seller's) perspective, giving the buyers the opportunity to fully inspect the house means that you've got nothing to hide. You've given the buyers every opportunity to check out the house for defects.

Later on, if something should crop up, you can always say that not only did you not know about it, the buyer's own inspector didn't find it. If the buyers have any complaints, they should take it up with the house inspector, not with you.

Recently, a friend sold a house which had a complete professional inspection. Later on, after the new buyers moved in, it turned out that the furnace had developed a leak in the heat exchanger. This is the part of the furnace where heated gas passes over a thin piece of metal and heats clean air that goes to the house. Any leak in the heat exchanger could introduce toxic fumes into the house. It's a serious health hazard and must be corrected before using the heater. A heat exchanger can cost upwards of $1200 and usually requires complete replacement of the furnace, which costs even more.

The buyers wanted my friend, the seller, to pay for a new furnace. The seller said it didn't leak when he owned the house. Further, the professional inspector passed the furnace. The inspector said the furnace was not leaking when he tried it out. The leak must have occurred after the sale.

Since it was an old furnace, my friend sent the buyers $250 toward replacement, while not admitting that he owed them anything. They accepted the amount and went ahead on their own to buy a new furnace.

It worked out fine. But what if there had been no professional inspector to say the furnace had not been leaking at the time of the sale?

The professional inspector's report can protect you as well as the buyer. It helps establish the true condition of the property at the time of the sale.

Be aware that inspection reports contain all sorts of caveats to protect the inspector. For example, they typically say that the inspection does not cover anything the inspector cannot see— under carpets, behind walls, in inaccessible areas, and so on. There are other disclaimers as well, often making the report seem to cover very little. On the other hand, how much can you expect an inspector to uncover in a 2-hour or so examination of a house?

Check out the www.ashi.com web site. This is the American Society of Home Inspectors, and it has a complete list of what an inspector should, and should not, look into as part of a professional inspection.

What If the Buyers Refuse to Have a Professional Inspection?

Normally, the buyers choose the inspector, order the professional inspection, and pay for it. But it is not usually a requirement of the purchase, unless the buyers make it so. You can suggest, even insist, that the buyers order the inspection. But you cannot force them to do so if they choose not to.

However, you can still achieve some protection for yourself by inserting a few lines into the purchase agreement that state that you have made the property available for a professional inspection and that you have encouraged the buyers to have one and that they have chosen not to do so. (Have a good attorney or agent draw up the language appropriate to your area.)

Later on, if a defect pops up and the buyers come back at you to fix or pay for it, you can always say, "Check the sales agreement. I told you to have an inspection, where this problem might have shown up, but you chose not to. Now, it's your headache."

No, that's not going to guarantee a buyer won't come after you to fix a problem. But it should help to ensure that the buyer won't have quite as solid a footing to stand on. And it might discourage a reasonable buyer from taking action against you. Of course, any reasonable buyer would have had the inspection to begin with.

Power Tip 38
Go with the Inspector

Most sellers think of having a home inspector come out as something akin to calling in a plumber to fix a leak. You show the plumber where the leak is and then leave and let him do his job. Later, he gives you the bill and you're ensured the leak is fixed.

A home inspection is nothing like that. Rather, it's like having a doctor probe your body for illness. You want to be there, giving the doctor symptoms and analyzing what he discovers. You want to be sure there are no misinterpretations, no mistakes. A home inspection is like that.

Go Along

Therefore, it is critical that you go along with the home inspector. As the seller, you can provide valuable information. An inspector might misunderstand something, and you can be right on the spot to correct him or her.

Further, for the same reason, you can expect any savvy buyer to go along with the inspector. The buyer will want to ask questions that the inspector can answer. You may be able to help out here, too.

> An inspector's oral comments are often far more revealing than the written report. The written report is typically filled with disclaimers. The verbal comments are far more off-the-cuff and revealing.

Here's what actually happened to me when I was selling a house a few years ago. The buyer's inspector showed up, in this case without the buyer. I said I wanted to go along, and the inspector agreed. (I've never had an inspector say the seller couldn't accompany him or her, except into areas that were dangerous to get into, such as the attic.)

The first thing the inspector found wrong was a bedroom wall that was on the other side of a bathroom. The wall had some apparent water stains on it, and the inspector jumped to the conclusion that the water was coming through the wall from a leaking shower stall on the other side. However, I was able to point out that my son had recently had a party in the room and what he was actually looking at were cola stains on the wall. A little bit of rubbing proved this to be the case.

The next problem, far more serious, was under the house. The house had a short 18-inch crawl space, and the joists were supported on wood piers standing on concrete footings. At each pier between the joist and the concrete footing was a metal screw bolt attaching them together.

"Looks like the house is slipping off its foundation, and you're trying to hold it in place," the inspector commented. "Might need a whole new foundation here."

I cringed. A new foundation on an existing house could cost upwards of $50,000.

"Not exactly, I explained. Those are earthquake retrofits. I had them installed to protect the house in case of a temblor."

The inspector nodded and we moved on. I figured I had just saved myself a sale, or at the least a lot of explanation and possibly money paid to the buyers for the "bad" foundation.

No, you may not have something as serious as this crop up. On the other hand, something else might. And you as the seller, who presumably knows the history of the house, can be there to give a reasonable explanation.

When There's a Real Problem

On the other hand, inspectors will often turn up real problems. Perhaps the water flow over the lot isn't from back to front (as it should be) but instead puddles under the house. The inspector may be able to suggest several solutions, including something as simple as a collector and a drain.

Or perhaps the water pressure is too high in the house. And the inspector notes that replacing a simple water-pressure control valve can solve the problem.

By going along with the inspector, not only can you see first hand what the problem is, if in fact there is one, but also you can often learn exactly what your options are in correcting it.

Later, when the buyer sees the inspection report and wants to have an expensive corrective procedure done, you can point out a much less expensive approach that the inspector suggested. In short, you may save yourself a ton of money and headaches by going with the inspector.

Wear Rough Clothing

It's important to understand that professional house inspectors go into some rather dirty and uncomfortable places. When I went under the house in the previous example, I spent a lot of time crawling on my back and belly. And under the house you can expect to run into all sorts of unfriendly creatures from spiders to rodents to standing water with mushrooms growing around it!

What this means is that you must dress appropriately and be ready for some roughing it. Usually, loose clothing that you are going to throw away anyhow works best. It should cover you all over.

> Beware: Going with the inspector is not for everyone. If you have any sort of medical or physical condition that could be affected by where you'll go, stay away. Get a friend or relative who's in better condition to go.

On the other hand, sometimes the areas can be dangerous. For example, if you go into the attic, you must be careful about standing on the rafters. Stand between them and you could fall right through the ceiling! (Usually, it's only thin sheetrock.)

Or, there might be insulation sprayed in the attic that requires you to wear a respirator. Or there could be lose asbestos from pipes or insulation.

Hopefully, a good inspector will prompt you with warnings before you get into a dangerous area. But even so, you should be aware that doing a house inspection does carry with it some risk.

Judging the Inspector

It's useful to come up with a sense of how good the inspector is. If you think the inspector is competent, you'll respect his or her report. On the other hand, if you suspect the inspector doesn't know what he or she is doing, you'll be far more inclined to argue about any apparent defects that are found.

When you go with the inspector, you'll have the opportunity to judge how professional he or she is. A good inspector will be prepared and will carry a flashlight, a long screwdriver for probing, and other tools. Be wary of an inspector who has to keep going back to the truck to get some tool he or she forgot.

> Professional inspectors should belong to national and state trade organizations. The two big national groups are American Society of Home Inspectors (ASHI) and National Association of Home Inspectors (NAHI). There are also local branches of these organizations.

I personally think some of the best professional house inspectors were former county building department inspectors. They are used to looking at construction and checking for problems. Of course, it's the buyer's choice in picking a professional inspector.

Power Tip 39
Negotiate Any Concessions
over a Found Defect

We all hope that the inspection report will turn up nothing serious, only minor defects. We're ready to deal with leaky faucets, broken sockets and plugs, and an occasional window screen that needs to be replaced. On the other hand, a serious crack in the foundation, a blown air conditioner, a roof that needs replacing, a sinkhole in the back yard, all these and other major problems are not welcome. But if they occur, they must be dealt with.

Give the Buyers an Explanation for
a Major Problem

The house inspector discovers that there are several long, wide cracks in the slab. (Many houses are constructed with a peripheral foundation and then a slab of concrete is essentially laid right on the ground—with an impermeable membrane beneath it to keep moisture out.) The buyers are very concerned about this. They are afraid that the house could fall down at some point in the future.

Prepare an explanation. If you didn't know the cracks were there, say so. Then indicate that you're willing to talk about corrective work, *if it is needed.*

This last point is very important. While there may be little disagreement about what a problem is, there can be significant differences of opinion about how to remedy it.

Cracked slabs, for example, are a matter of much debate. There are some who say that the only real method of fixing them is to lift up the house, remove the original slab, and pour a new one. The cost could easily exceed $30,000, even for a modest-sized house.

On the other extreme are those who say to simply ignore the cracks. Assuming that steel rebars (reinforcement bars) or at least wire mesh was laid in the concrete, it's not likely going anywhere. The metal will keep it from shifting, and the best thing you can do with the cracks is to ignore them.

On the middle ground are those who recommend patching the cracks. They often cut into the concrete, drill holes inserting new rebar, and then patch over with concrete. This process costs only a few thousand dollars, but it involves removing furniture and floor covering and is quite messy.

> My own opinion is that if the cracks are not particularly big and the slab has been there for a couple of decades and it has lots of rebar, chances are it's not going to move much more. I've ignored such cracks in slabs in houses I've bought, while paying special attention to groundwater diversion to avoid causing any future cracks. On the other hand, if there's no rebar (or wire mesh) and the cracks are offsetting (one side higher than the other), then I believe corrective work should be done to fix them.

What you need to do is to present several opinions from reputable sources. Get a couple of contractors who specialize in the field in there to see what they think. Dig up some literature on the subject from the Internet or from books. In short, learn as much as you can and try to educate the buyer as well. Many times, when both parties take a closer look, they decide that there isn't such a big problem after all.

Most initial negotiations are over three areas

Areas of Negotiation

1. *Is there really a problem?* Did the inspector goof or maybe it's not something that anyone needs to worry about?
2. *How can it be corrected?* As seen in the earlier example of a cracked slab, solutions range from doing nothing to replacing the entire slab. You need to reach agreement with the buyers over what needs to be done.
3. *Who should pay for it?* This is usually the trickiest area, with the buyer saying you should pay for it all and, if you're like most sellers, your saying it's up to the buyer to foot the bill.

Paying for Fixing the Problem

Once both you and the buyers agree that there's a problem that needs a remedy, negotiations can begin on who's going to pay for the work. I find that a usage formula is helpful here. It depends on how much use a person has of the property and works something like this.

Deciding Who Pays

- *If it's going to cost under $1000.* Just pay for it yourself. It's a small amount, given the overall sales price of most houses, and it's simply easier to pay to have the problem go away than to waste time and energy, and possibly blow a deal, over it.

- *If the property is less than 10 years old.* Call the builder. Most builders warrant the houses they construct for up to 10 years. They may have insurance to cover the problem if it's a serious defect such as a broken foundation or bad roof. On the other hand, they won't help if it's a maintenance problem such as a leaky water heater or furnace. Contact the manufacturer in this case.

- *If you've lived in the house for a long time.* Consider paying for most of it yourself. Chances are what's involved here is deferred maintenance. It's often something you should have corrected while you lived there but didn't. Yes, you can always refuse to pay. But consider, maybe it's something you really ought to pay.

- *If you've lived there a short time.* On the other hand, if you've lived in the house for only 5 years, yet it's 30 years old and needs a new roof, why should you pay for the entire roof? Point out to the buyer that you didn't have 30 years of benefit for the old roof. And further, the buyer will presumably have the benefit of the new roof for the next 30 years. Consider agreeing to patch the old roof but not putting on a new one. If this doesn't work, offer to contribute only a small amount to the new roof, say 25 percent of the cost. Only if you can't make the deal any other way and don't want to risk losing it should you pay for most or all of the cost.

- *If the house is very old.* Old houses have problems. Sometimes those problems are severe. Any buyer should realize this. Unless you're selling the house for top dollar claiming that you've completely refurbished it, expect the buyer to pay for or assume the burden for much of any major fix-up work.

Negotiate, Negotiate, Negotiate

In real estate everything is always up for grabs. Sometimes buyers recoup in negotiations over defects all the ground they gave up when agreeing to price. Sometimes sellers get away with murder by not having to fix major problems. It all depends on how good you are at negotiation.

You may want to look into my book, *Tips & Traps When Negotiating Real Estate*, McGraw-Hill, 1995.

Don't make the mistake of thinking that the negotiations end when the sales agreement is signed. Often that's just the beginning. The real negotiations may take place over defects found in the property.

Power Tip 40
Do Some Fix-Up Work
Yourself

When there's fix-up work to do because of revelations from disclosures or an inspection report, some sellers immediately think about doing it themselves. If you're at all handy, you feel that you can save substantial sums of money by doing the work on your own.

You can save money. And many people do successfully cure fix-up problems. On the other hand, you can also jump from the frying pan into the fire. You have to be very careful about what you choose to do, and what you hire out.

What Does the Buyer Demand?

Often, it's a matter of what the negotiations involve

For example, there's water damage in two adjacent bathrooms. The floors and subfloors have to be replaced along with some drywall along the walls. The buyers want you to pay for it, and you discover that it's going to cost around $1500. However, since it's mostly labor intensive, you figure that the materials will only cost around $300. So you agree to have the work done, provided you can do it yourself. Will the buyers go along?

Some buyers will. They just want the work done, the problem fixed. However, savvy buyers will know that sellers rarely are capable of doing truly professional work. Hence, they may insist that licensed workers do all work. That means you'll have to pay the big bucks.

On the other hand, maybe your buyer is one who doesn't care. The question now becomes, *should* you do the work yourself? How do you decide if it makes sense for you to handle it on your own?

Does It Make Sense for You to Do It?

There are a number of factors you will want to consider in making your decision:

Deciding on Whether to Do the Work Yourself

1. *Does it involve hazardous or dangerous work?* If the work requires tackling gas lines of any kind, *always* hire it out. The only exception would be if you're a licensed plumber yourself. The reason is simply that you don't want to mess with the liability. To a slightly lesser extent, the same holds true with electrical and plumbing work.

If you do any work on gas lines, electrical or other critical house systems, and later, after the sale, those systems fail, causing a fire or other damage, particularly where people are injured, you could be held liable. That's why you want to pay to have a professional do this work.

2. *Does it involve heavy lifting?* Most people can handle installing drywall. However, each sheet weighs as much as 100 pounds or more. If you're a weekend warrior when it comes to doing handy man jobs and you're a bit out of shape, you'll save money by having a professional do it—just think of the doctor bills!

3. *Can you do a good job?* The classic example here is working with stucco, the cement material used as an external covering for many houses. Sometimes there are broken areas and cracks in stucco that must be patched. Many house owners, realizing that what we're talking about here is slapping some cement onto a wall, feel they can easily tackle it themselves. Yes, it is a bit heavy, but not overly so. Yes, it is messy, but they can handle that. And they can certainly handle not paying a big fee to have it done.

All of these are good reasons. However, the biggest concern of all has to be appearance. How will the finished product look? If you can patch stucco and come out with a professional-looking job that matches the rest of the house, then by all means, consider doing it yourself. On the other hand, if your work will look like a poorly done patch, then hire it out. Chances are that when the buyers see it, they won't approve it and you'll have to have a professional come in, rip your work out, and do it right. All of which will cost even more money!

4. *Do you have the time?* Chances are you already have a full-time job and really don't need another. Yet, when you begin tackling fix-up jobs on a house, you enter the realm of time-consuming work. Don't simply consider just the time it takes to do the actual job. Think of the time it takes to go to the store and get materials, and then to go back to get the elbow or wire or whatever that you forgot. And then take however long you think it will take you to do the job and multiply by three. That's the additional time it will take because you're aren't familiar with the task and need to redo it several times to get it right.

On the other hand, how much is your time worth?

Think of it as if you were taking time off from your job; how much would it be worth to you? Even if it's your leisure time, working on the house means you can't be relaxing. All of which is to say that time is money, and your time is valuable. If you spend it fixing a problem on the house, you can't spend it working or relaxing elsewhere. What is that cost? Is it worth it, now, to do the job on the house?

5. *Do you have the tools?* There's an old maxim that goes, "There's the right tool for every job." If you don't have that right tool, then you'll either have to buy it or have to improvise with what you've got. If you buy it, you're adding to your costs...and besides, chances are you'll never need that specialized tool again! If you improvise with what you've got, you stand the risk of doing a poor job.

Will It Need to Be Inspected?

Some work requires building department approval and that means inspections to see if it was done correctly. Any work involving electrical, plumbing, heating, or major structural changes usually requires a permit.

Keep in mind that building department inspectors tend to be especially rough on home owners doing their own work. This is not to say that inspectors don't take the time to explain what needs to be done and how. My experience is that they bend over backwards to be helpful. It's just that they are also very critical because they suspect (sometimes rightly so!) that the owner may not always know exactly what he or she is doing.

Can You Get a Permit?

Maybe not. My experience has been that building departments will usually allow an owner to do his or her own work, provided they intend to live in the property in the future. Often the building department will require that you sign a statement that you plan on living in the house for the next 6 months to 1 year as a condition of getting a permit. This is to ensure that no one else is threatened by shoddy work that you might do. On the other hand, some areas require that electrical and plumbing be done only by a licensed contractor.

Further, if you're planning on selling soon, you may not be able to secure a permit. The building department may politely, but firmly, say, "no." This is more likely the case with anything dealing with gas, electrical, or plumbing work.

Should You Do Any of It?

Of course you should. I do. However, you should avoid doing anything involving liability. You should also avoid doing work that's over your head, as evidenced by the five questions noted earlier. On the other hand, if you're competent, have the time and inclination, go for it!

9

Control the Escrow

Power Tip 41
Choose the Escrow and Title
Company Carefully

There's an old adage in real estate that goes to the effect that the person who controls the escrow controls the deal. It's not far off, and in the next tip we'll more clearly see why. Here, however, we're going to look at escrow and title companies from the perspective of cost and reliability.

Plan on having an escrow company handle the closing for you. On the East Coast this is sometimes handled by attorneys; however, for the most part escrow companies do the work. And escrow companies are often affiliated with title insurance companies. If you have any choice in the matter, and you very well may, choose your escrow and title insurance companies very carefully. It could save a bundle of headaches and money.

What Do Escrow and Title
Insurance Companies Do?

An *escrow company* is a stakeholder. It's like a neutral third party who holds all the documents and money and awaits word that all the requirements of the sales agreement have been carried out. When the third party learns that they have, it gives title to the new buyers and your cash to you.

A *title insurance company* checks title to your the property. In the form of a "prelim" or preliminary report, it lets you know if there are any "clouds" on the title. These are encumbrances, usually liens that must be paid before clear title can be given. A typical lien would be from a creditor who got a judgment against you. Perhaps you forgot to pay it. Or maybe your were angry and decided not to pay it. Either way, it must now be paid (or the creditor must otherwise be assuaged) for you to get clear title. When the company determines that the title is clear, it ensures that title to the buyer (and depending on the policy obtained) to the lender.

Who Pays for Escrow Services and
Title Insurance?

That's up to local custom. In some areas the buyer pays the entire cost. In other areas the sellers pays. In many areas the costs are split. Usually, if there's a separate lender's escrow and title insurance, called an American Land Title Association (ALTA), it's paid for by the buyer.

> Who pays for what is another matter for negotiation. There's nothing to say you can't pay for the buyer's title and escrow costs or that the buyer can't pay for yours. It's up for negotiation when you sell your house.

All Services Are Not Alike

A number of years ago, all escrow and title insurance costs were pretty much similar. The companies all did the same functions, hence their prices were similar.

In recent years, however, there have been huge disparities between different escrow companies and different title companies. Today, for example, it is possible for one escrow company's charges to be as much as twice as high as those of another. Since these charges are largely unregulated (or what regulations there are tend to be laxly enforced), it's possible to pay a lot or a little, depending on how carefully you shop.

How Do I Know the Costs?

If you're going to be the one to pay for escrow and title insurance, then you'd do well to take a little time to investigate what your costs will be. Get a list of different companies offering these services in your area. Any agent should be able to provide this. Lenders can likewise offer it. As a last resort, simply check under "escrow" and "title insurance" in the Yellow Pages of your local phone book.

Then make a few calls. It's usually not necessary to actually go down to the companies, as you should be able to determine most of what you need to know by phone. Call and ask to speak to an escrow or title insurance officer. Describe the deal you have, including:

- The price of the property.
- The size of the loan and the buyer's lender (if you know).

- Any unusual costs such as separate lender's escrow and title insurance.
- When the escrow is scheduled to close.

The officer should be able to give you a pretty accurate estimate of the costs involved.

> Reputation is also important. Ask a few agents (who you undoubtedly met in the course of selling your house) about any escrow and title insurance company you're interested in. Find out if they have been sticking to their initial cost estimates. Find out if there have been any other problems with them.

There usually isn't any concern with title insurance companies since they normally are local branches of huge national organizations. It won't hurt, however, to check out the parent company's ratings.

With escrow companies, it's a bit different. Sometimes they are a part of a huge title insurance company. Other times they are nothing more than a mom and pop operation out of a garage. If it's the latter, think twice before trusting your money to them. Yes, they probably are licensed by the state, but that won't help if they go bankrupt or abscond with your money!

Be Careful of Agent's and Buyer's Demands

Sometimes you'll be told you have no choice in who handles the escrow. Usually, it's the agent who tells you this, particularly if the agent is from a large franchise company. These companies are sometimes affiliated with escrow and title insurance companies. There may be an unwritten rule in the company that agents are to send business to the affiliate.

This type of activity is unethical, if not downright illegal. Nevertheless, if you (or the buyer's) agent says, "We're using XYZ escrow, you don't have a choice," you may be hard pressed to refuse; you won't want to risk the deal.

Nevertheless, you can, indeed, refuse. You can say that if you're paying for it, you want the cheapest, and the agent's company be damned. This may produce some consternation, but in order to preserve the deal, you may get your way. After all, in almost all cases, remember that the agent doesn't get paid until the deal closes. In the process of choosing your title company, you could save yourself thousands of dollars! (You may not have a choice—federal regulations in some cases prohibit the seller from choosing the escrow/title company. Check with your agent to see if they apply in your case.)

Reusing the Same Companies

Often, you'll get a significant discount (around 25 percent) if you use the same title company you used when you bought your house, provided not more than a few years have elapsed. A smaller discount may be obtained from an escrow company for the same reason.

But be wary. A buyer might want to determine the escrow and title company for the same reason!

Power Tip 42
Have Escrow Report to You
Constantly

As noted in the last tip, the person who controls escrow controls the deal. The reason is that escrow can often make or break a transaction. It can facilitate getting the various must-do chores accomplished, or it can set up roadblocks that keep the deal from closing.

If you select the escrow company, the escrow officers will tend to report to you. You want to encourage this behavior as much as possible. Indeed, you want to let it be known that you're to be called as soon as any problem of any kind surfaces. And you want certain other items to be tracked on a weekly, if not daily, basis.

What we're talking about here are three big areas:

- The buyer's efforts at getting financing
- The buyer's removal of contingencies
- Clearing the title of any clouds

All of these areas must be dealt with if escrow is to close and your house is to sell. If problems develop in one that aren't resolved, you could end up with a no-sale.

What If Someone Else Controls Escrow?

Let's say that instead of the escrow officer reporting to you, he or she reports to the buyer's agent. And the buyer is having trouble getting financing. Indeed, the buyer's first lender has refused to go forward with a mortgage, and now the buyer is scrambling trying to find a second lender.

None of the customary paperwork from the lender is coming into escrow, which is an immediate warning sign. The escrow officer reports this to the buyer's agent, who well knows the problem. But, it is not reported to you. And you feel happy and content thinking things are moving along just fine.

You've got a 45-day escrow and when you reach the last week, you call the escrow officer to be sure the deal is ready to close. The escrow officer says that, yes, it will close, as soon as the lender gets the appropriate documents in.

Sounds fine, right? Until it's the next to last day and you call to see if the buyer's have signed off on their mortgage. You call and the escrow officer reports again that as soon as the lender's documents are in, preparations for closing can be made.

Suddenly, you become alarmed—preparations for closing? It's the next to last day! What do you mean "as soon as?" Why aren't the documents in? The escrow officer says blandly, "I'm merely a neutral third party. Check with the buyers or their agent."

You do and discover that, after much scrambling, the buyers can't get financing. They have no lender. However, they would like you to extend escrow for another 45 days in the wan hope that maybe they can find some lender who'll finance their deal.

Of course, you quash that. The deal's blown. Because there's no loan, the buyers get their deposit back. But you now have to go through the whole process of getting your house back on the market.

Chances are you've lost a month or more of precious selling time. On the other hand, if you had been informed of the buyer's problems in securing financing early on, you could have taken appropriate steps to get your house exposed to other buyers in a more timely fashion. (Particularly if you had limited the financing contingency by saying that you could continue to show the property until the buyers had a firm commitment from a lender.)

When There Are Contingency or Title Problems

Similarly, you need to be informed as soon as the buyers have approved the termite, house inspection, and other reports and disclosures. Typically, these are signed off on and turned into escrow. If you don't know for sure that contingencies have been removed, you might simply assume they have, particularly if you didn't hear anything to the contrary. You might have no deal, yet be sitting there for weeks thinking you do!

And, if there's a problem with the title on your end, you need to know as soon as possible in order to resolve it. You want the escrow officer to call and let you know that there's a 13-year old lien recorded against your property for $300 in favor of a credit company. You can't get it removed unless, and until, you learn of it.

Losing Documents

Perhaps the worst thing that an escrow officer can do is to lose critical documents. You get a signed release for a lien and send it in and the deal's ready to close. Only the escrow officer can't find the document. So, unless you had the foresight to get a notarized copy, you've got to go through the whole process of getting the release again, something that could take weeks.

This could have the effect of costing you the deal since you wouldn't be able to close on time. Or it could delay closing. Sometimes, coincidentally when the buyer's control escrow, this may coincide with extra time they need to get financing.

I found that when I control escrow, there are seldom any lost documents, at least those that would aversely affect me.

Managing the Escrow

It's important to understand that someone from your side, either you or your agent, needs to stay on top of things. Even if you control escrow, this manager needs to be calling the escrow officer regularly to be sure that everything is moving along with the sign-off of contingencies, the buyers' getting funding, and the clearing of title. You can't expect the escrow officer, who may be handling dozens if not hundreds of deals, to watch everything for you every minute.

Nevertheless, a good escrow officer will have a little book or chart or computer program with dates on it when certain things are due. And he or she will call you when a date is missed. Similarly, you'll get a call if something comes in early.

Drawing Up the Escrow Instructions

Finally, there's the matter of the escrow instructions themselves. When escrow is opened, you (or whoever opens it) will present the escrow officer with the signed sales agreement. The officer will read it over and will then prepare instructions to escrow that will fulfill all the terms of the agreement. You and the buyers will then be asked to sign identical pairs of instructions, and escrow will begin moving forward.

While most escrow instructions are straightforward, there are usually a few areas open to interpretation. For example, exactly what did

you and the buyer mean when you wrote in, "buyer to approve seller's repairs of ceiling damage." Does the buyer have the right to
refuse approval? Must the buyer approve your repairs no matter
what? The instructions will usually clarify this.

> Vague language is the bane of sales agreements. That's why you
> should always have a good agent or attorney write in any terms.
> While it might seem perfectly clear to you, and perhaps to the
> buyer, unless the language is precise, later on it might be diffi-
> cult to say what really was meant.

Be sure that you read over the escrow instructions carefully and
that the interpretation of what was meant by the sales agreement is
accurate. If you don't control escrow, beware of instructions that
end up favoring the buyer. After all, if it's up to the escrow officer to
interpret what was meant, and if he or she is listening to what the
buyers (or the buyers' agent) have to say, the interpretation could
be slanted in their favor. On the other hand, if you have the escrow
officer's ear, it's likely to go the way you remember it.

> Be sure to have a good agent or attorney check over any parts
> of the escrow instructions that you aren't clear about. The
> instructions form the basis of closing the deal. Yes, the ruling
> document is probably going to be the sales agreement if litiga-
> tion occurs. Nevertheless, as a practical matter, the escrow
> instructions are what you must stick to in order to get the deal
> closed in a timely fashion. Be sure they are correct.

Power Tip 43
Resolve Escrow Problems
Quickly

Procrastination has become fashionable in some parts of our society. Conveniently forgetting the time for a party and showing up late (a kind of procrastination) is trendy. Pop-psychology gurus sometimes describe procrastination as a way of dealing with certain problems, "If you just forget about, it often will go away."

However, when it comes to closing a real estate transaction, procrastination is the worst possible choice of action. Things don't go away; they just get worse.

The Meaning of a Deadline

I once knew an author who had a very blasé attitude toward deadlines. He said something to the effect that, "Deadlines are simply there to push you to get organized. They aren't brick walls. If you miss them by a month or two, the world won't end. The idea is to get the best possible product, not get it done on time."

Maybe that's true with literary works, but it certainly isn't true when closing a real estate deal. Every sales agreement that I've ever seen calls for a set time to close escrow. It might be 30 days, 45 days, 2 weeks, or whatever. But on a certain date, escrow is to close. That's a deadline fixed in stone. If it doesn't close, there could be dire consequences.

If escrow doesn't close on time, then there may be no deal. Missing the deadline may allow the buyer to simply take his or her deposit and look elsewhere. Similarly, it could allow you, the seller, to wash your hands of the deal and look for a different buyer. Miss the deadline for closing escrow and you stand an excellent chance of losing the deal.

If escrow doesn't close on time and both parties are agreeable, the deadline can be extended. However, often one or the other will see an advantage in dumping the deal by refusing an extension. (Some sales agreements give the agent the power to extend escrow usually for up to a month.)

What Holds Up Escrow

Almost anything can slow escrow down and cause it to miss its closing date. Here are the three most common problems:

Most Common Problems That Hold Up Escrow

Clouds on the Title   This is something that is up to you to correct. You were in an auto accident 12 years ago and were sued by the other party. You lost and the court awarded $1200 against you. When you were asked for the money, you told the other person to take a big flying leap.

So, that other person got a court judgment and then filed a lien against your house. It's been sitting there, quietly, for 12 years, a long enough time for you to completely forget about it. Now, however, when you want to sell, the title insurance company uncovers the problem. It won't give clear title until this lien is removed. Like it or not, that means you'll probably have to pay it off. But to do that, you must locate whom to pay it to and then, once payment is made, get them to record a release.

It's been 12 years now, and it's hard to find the other party. They've moved several times and forwarding addresses have been sketchy. In fact, after pursuing this for a few days, you discover that you really can't find them at all! What are you to do?

If you waited until the last minute, you very likely are up the creek without a paddle. The escrow officer might be willing to withhold $1200 from your payment and close. On the other hand, depending on how the lien was written, the title insurance company might not allow that. In other words, you might not be able to close.

If, however, you started early, you could get a "quiet title" action to remove the lien. Here, you go to court, and the court can issue a release. It probably would allow withholding the money for a certain time, pending location of the appropriate parties. But a quiet title action takes time. You only have that time if you act early.

A Problem Lender   Some lenders act timely. Others are notoriously delinquent. These "bad" lenders take forever to fully approve the buyers. Then they ask for all sorts of documents that are difficult to come by (such as naturalization papers, divorce documents, old tax returns, and so on). They may even demand a new appraisal on the property. Finally, when everything is supposedly set, they take forever to issue their own documents, sometimes lose them so they must be issued a second or even third time, and then are slow about funding the money. In short, they do everything possible to delay things.

As we noted in the last tip, you will want to have these problems reported to you as soon as possible. But then, as soon as you hear about them, you need to act upon them. Call the buyers and their agent and see if you can help. Prod them to keep up on things. Sometimes buyers move quickly, other times they seem to just plod along. If you get a plodder, it may be up to you to put pressure on to get that loan funded. You may also find yourself making calls to the lender.

> Normally, a lender will only talk to the borrower, but in closing a real estate transaction, strange things happen and the buyers' lender may sometimes be willing to talk to you when things are slowed down, letting you know what documents are missing. It won't hurt to ask.

Problems with Physical Fixes These are normally your responsibility, and you have to jump right on them if you want escrow to close on time. For example, you've agreed to put in a French drain to direct rainwater away from the house. How hard can that be? It's a trench 12 to18 inches deep, with some 4-inch pipe laid down in it.

So you procrastinate and put it off until a week before escrow is scheduled to close. Then you find you can't get a crew to come out and dig the hole. So you dig it yourself, only to break a gas line leading to the house. Now you've got to hire a plumber. And there needs to be a building inspection, which uncovers the fact that the underground gas line wasn't properly wrapped with protective plastic when it was first laid. The city wants you to rip out the gas line from the street to the house and replace it. If you've only got a week when you start, you might as well kiss the deal goodbye. You've probably got 2 to 3 weeks (or more) of work there. On the other hand, if you began early, you'll have the time to finish.

Act Quickly

The whole point here is that you're up against a deadline with escrow. If this is your first time through (or the first time in quite a while), chances are you won't know or remember which things are likely to take a long time to do and which can be done swiftly. Therefore, the best advice is to act on everything immediately.

> Ask your escrow officer and your agent to help you prepare a list of everything you will possibly need to do to close escrow. Then start work on it immediately.

Power Tip 44
Set a Move-Out Date

Sellers are always uncomfortable about when they should actually move out of the house. If you're in the process of buying another house and the purchase doesn't hinge on the sale of the old property, you may be able to set a move-out date long in advance. Then, whether your old property sells or not, on that day you're gone.

More commonly, however, you want to move in an orderly fashion, but you don't want to move until you're sure the sale is going to go through. You don't want to be making payments on two houses. So how do you know when to set the move-out date?

The Critical Events

There are certain critical events in the sale of a house that give you an indication of when you'll need to be out of the house:

Events That Indicate When You'll Need to Move

- *You sign a sales agreement, and it calls for a 45-day escrow.* You can feel fairly sure that you'll need to be out in a month and a half. However, just because you signed off on the deal, doesn't mean it will close or, as we've seen, that it will close on time.

- *The buyers remove the last major contingency (not including the financing contingency which often remains in force until the sale is concluded).* If you have a 45-day escrow and on day 15 the buyers approve the last contingency by removing it, you should start packing in earnest. This suggests that the deal is definitely going to close and on time.

- *The buyers mortgage funds.* When the money is in the bank (or at least ready to be used to pay for the house), the closing is only a day or two away. You should not only be packed, but the movers should be showing up.

- *The escrow closes.* Typically, a sales agreement calls for possession to be given to buyers "upon close of escrow." That means when the deal closes, the buyers are going to be showing up with their moving truck, so you want to be sure you're out of there.

Possession can be given to the buyers at any time mutually agreed upon, before, upon, or after close of escrow.

Coordinating Your Move with the Buyers

Once it becomes clear that the deal is going to close, you should call the buyers (if they don't call you first) and make some common arrangements for moving. For example, the deal may be closing on a Wednesday, but because of work responsibilities, you can't move any time except on the weekend. So, should you move the weekend before escrow closes (not knowing for sure that it will close) or the weekend after?

My suggestion is to ask the buyer for a few days and move the weekend after. (Better to be safe than sorry with regard to a closing.) If it's only a day or two, chances are the buyers will simply agree, particularly since they probably aren't planning to move until that weekend anyway. However, if you're both planning on moving the same weekend, be sure you're out by Saturday night so they can move in on Sunday.

Some buyers are very strict and may charge you 2 or 3 days rent if you stay beyond the close of escrow. This is always negotiable and usually is a small sum of money. If the buyers insist, pay it. Just chalk it up as a moving expense.

What About Moving Arrangements?

Make these well in advance. You'll want to be sure that you include each of the items noted in the following list. The general rule is to make arrangements assuming that you'll move on a certain day, even if you're not certain that the deal will closely in a timely fashion. The reason is that it's usually far easier to get movers and utilities to delay a few days or move up the date a few days than it is to

get them to set a date. Setting a date requires putting you into the
system, and that can take time.

Moving Arrangements to Make

1. *Movers.* Your choice is usually between hiring a moving company
   and hiring a truck and doing it yourself. If you can at all afford it,
   I suggest using movers. While it may cost a bit more, you'll probably make it up on doctors' visits and medications that you won't
   need because you didn't strain yourself doing your own move.
   Besides, renting a one-way moving truck these days is quite
   expensive. If you haven't done this for a while, check out the
   costs; you could be in for a shock. Movers usually have two rates—
   local moves are based on so much an hour (around $65 to $100
   an hour in most urban areas as of this writing). Long distance is
   based on weight. The more weight you transport, the costlier it is.
   All movers offer insurance, but it's expensive and from reports
   I've received, difficult to collect if there's a problem. There's
   been a lot of reports of shoddy practices in the moving industry,
   so try to get a major moving company. Also, look for recommendations from a friend or an associate.

2. *New house arrangements.* If you're buying another house, try to
   arrange it so that the escrows close at the same time. That way you
   won't have double payments. If, however, that can't be done, try
   to arrange it so that the house you're buying closes shortly before
   the house you're selling. You'll have some double payments, but
   you'll also have a few days to get into the new place and fix it up
   a bit before you move in. If the new house closes after the first,
   and you can't arrange with the buyers of your house to allow you
   to live in it for a while longer, you may have to move twice—once
   to a temporary house, such as a motel, and a second time to your
   new house. That's not a very desirable way to handle the move.

3. *Arrange for the utilities.* You're going to need to transfer or estab-
   lish at least the following:
   - Water
   - Gas
   - Electric
   - TV (cable)

- Newspapers
- Garbage pickup
- Phone
- Gardening service
- Schools (getting your children enrolled)

Try to arrange for these at least a month in advance. If you're moving to a new area with a different utility provider, you may need to put up a deposit to establish your account. It could take several weeks before it's all set up and you're given a day for "turn-on." Remember, once you've got your turn-on date, you can postpone it fairly easily. Thus, get the utilities set up early and then, if necessary, change the date around to suit your move.

Power Tip 45
Restrict Buyer's Demands for
a Final Walk-Through

What we're talking about here is the common practice today of allowing the buyer to walk through the house one last time just before signing the escrow papers to approve the property. The great danger, as we'll see shortly, is that the buyer will use this final walk-through as an opportunity to try to back out of the deal. (This tip could just as easily have gone into the section on negotiation in Chapter 7. However, since the final walk-through occurs at the very end of escrow, I've put it here where you're most likely to think about it.)

Why Have a Final Walk-Through?

The final walk-through is designed to avoid problems after the sale is concluded. In the past, before these were commonplace, buyers would take possession of the property and then discover, to their horror, that it wasn't at all what they had been shown a month earlier when they had made their offer. Common buyers complaints follow:

Common Buyers Complaints with No Walk-Through

- The sellers had allowed the place to get run down, not maintaining it in a good manner. The lawns and gardens hadn't been watered, the rugs were filthy, there were stains on the walls, and so on.

> Some sellers would decide that, once there was a sale, it was party time in the old house. Long orgy-style parties would occur that would literally destroy the paint, wallpaper, and flooring. These sellers felt that it was the buyer's concern. With a buyer's walk-through, however, this problem has largely been eliminated.

- Missing items. The sellers had removed chandeliers, wall coverings, floor coverings, appliances, or whatever, all discovered only when the buyers took possession. Again, a walk-through avoids this problem since the buyers get to see the property *before* they sign off and get to bring problems to the seller's attention.

- Broken items. The stove doesn't work. There's a cracked window. The fan in the hallway won't turn on, and so on. Finding these before the buyer moves in allows them to be corrected by the closing date.

Is a Walk-Through Helpful for the Seller?

From the preceding discussion, it might seem that the walk-through only benefits the buyer. It lets the buyer go through the house and make demands on the seller that are, in effect, "fix this or clean that or I won't buy."

Yes, that's sort of true. However, these demands are likely to be there whether they occur during the walk-through or after the sale. And if they are reasonable, you should plan on doing them. After all, if you made the house dirty, you'll need to clean it. If you sold a house with broken appliances, you'll have to fix them. And so forth.

However, it's much more costly to fix something *after* the sale. After the sale, the buyer usually determines who's going to do the fixing. And since you're paying, it's usually the highest-priced professional.

Before the sale is concluded, however, you can call in the cut-rate professional to do the job. Or, depending on what's involved, you can do it yourself sometimes for virtually nothing. In addition, because you're right there on the spot, you can see to it that the work is done properly. If you're just the wallet after the sale, you have to rely on the buyer to be sure it's done right or possibly pay to have it done again.

In short, for items that really must be cleaned or fixed by you, the seller, the final walk-through does provide a service.

Finally, there's the matter of missing things. Usually, this is a matter of interpretation. You feel the chandelier's yours; the buyers thought it came with the house.

There's usually some negotiation involved here. And, again, it's usually easier to do this before you move (and while you can replace the item yourself, if necessary) while you're still living there.

As noted earlier, it's better to remove and replace any items of personal property you want to take with you before you show the house to buyers. What buyers don't see, they won't want.

When the Buyer Uses the Walk-Through to Get Out of the Purchase

This is a much more serious concern. What if the buyer, after walking through the house 2 days before escrow is to close, says something like, "That's not how I remember it. I thought the house was bigger, brighter, with more carpeting, and better appliances. I don't want it now."

Can the buyer actually get out of the deal? Maybe.

It all depends on how the walk-through contingency was written. In years past the final walk-through was a simple contingency statement, usually written in such a way as to state that the purchase was subject to the buyer giving approval of the premises in a final inspection to be held within 3 days of closing. In theory, if the buyer doesn't give approval, there's no deal.

In practice, it could lead to all kinds of trouble, including litigation. And the outcome there is always going to be uncertain.

To avoid the problem, many brokers have taken to beefing up the final walk-through. Today, many purchase contracts state that the buyer has the right to inspect the property within 3 days of closing for the sole purpose of determining that it is in the same condition as it was when the buyer was first shown the house. Further, such contracts often include wording to the effect that the final walk-through is not intended to give the buyer an opportunity to back out of the deal.

This wording, which you should look for in your sales contract, may help. Nevertheless, what if the buyer says that house isn't as it was before? Now it becomes a matter of proving what was and what wasn't. Again, if it gets to litigation, it can easily become a real mess.

What's important to keep sight of is that you're likely to have two kinds of buyers. One kind is the checker who is going to going to still want to buy the house and the worst that's likely to happen is that there will be a couple of complaints about this or that, things which you will very likely find easy to correct. This buyer will simply check things out.

The other buyer is the destroyer, the one who wants to destroy the deal in the worst way. (Perhaps this buyer has found a house he or she likes better or has decided not to move or whatever.) The destroyer is going to find all sorts of things wrong and never be satisfied. There will be scrapes and broken items and tears and things that were changed and on and on. As soon as you correct one problem, three more are created. Unless you have a videotaped recording of the property exactly as it was before (and even if you have this), it's going to be hard to demonstrate that the house is exactly as it was when first shown to the buyer.

After a point, with a determined destroyer, you come to realize that either this is going to end up in court *or* you're simply going to say, "Okay, you're not worth the hassle. Take your deposit and go." If the market is hot and there are buyers aplenty, you may be better off doing this. On the other hand, if the market's cold, this is the only buyer in 6 months, and you're desperate to get out, you may want check with your attorney.

10
Save on Closing Costs

Power Tip 46
Strike a Deal with Your Agent

As I've said before, everything in real estate is negotiable, so why not the commission as well? Indeed, the commission is negotiable. Does that mean you'll get it cut? Sometimes. You won't know, however, unless you ask.

The real trick is to know when to ask the agent to cut the commission and the reason to give. You increase your chances significantly if you know when and why.

When Is an Agent Likely to Cut the Commission?

There are four times in a transaction that an agent is likely to cut the commission. We'll look at each separately.

Times When an Agent Might Cut the Commission

1. *When you list the property.* There is no official listing rate. Although 6 percent seems to be the most commonly used rate, it could just as easily be 5, 7, or any other percentage. You can negotiate this when you initially sign your listing. Some agents, of course, will not accept less than what they feel is their own going rate (what they charge everyone). Others will have a lower going rate or will agree to accept less than their going rate. You have to ask and show determination. Of course, you don't want to hire an agent who accepts a lower rate, but then doesn't work hard for you. Check out Tip 9 for more help here.

2. *When your agent also represents the buyer.* Usually, there are two agents to each transaction, one for you, the seller, and another for the buyer. But there's no reason that the same agent can't represent both. When this happens, the agent is actually collecting the entire commission. Instead of getting half the commission or, for example 3 percent, the agent is getting the full 6 percent. You can ask the agent to help you get more of your equity into your pocket by reducing the commission.

If you want to renegotiate the commission rate after you've already signed the listing agreement, you should do it *before* you agree to the sales contract. Most sales contracts specify the commission rate and to whom it is to be paid. Get the agent to lower the rate on the contract, and you've saved yourself the money. However, once you sign the sales contract, you're usually locked in.

3. *When your selling agent finds you your next house.* Here you have the agent getting a full commission again. However, instead of representing both you and the buyer of your house, here the agent represents you when you sell and when you buy your next house. The agent, in effect, gets half of two commissions. You can ask the agent to help you with a reduction in the commission amount.

Many agents are amenable to such a request, provided it is presented properly. The time to do it is either when you sign or when you are negotiating the sales agreement. Point out to the agent that you intend on buying your next house through him or her, provided the agent can help you out with the commission. Agents are business people and you're offering to increase their business. You're asking for a reduced rate for two deals. Your chances of getting a concession, here, are excellent.

Note: You'll probably get the reduction when you purchase the next property. Otherwise, you might simply take the reduced commission money from the sale of your old and then not use the agent to purchase your new one.

4. *When you're selling a high-priced house.* Many people have asked if an agent really works, for example, five times harder to sell a $1 million house than a $200,000 house. Probably the liability is greater should something go wrong. And the agent must cater to a different clientele, usually meaning buying a more expensive car, dress, office, and so forth. Nevertheless, the selling process is essentially the same.

As a consequence, sellers of very high-priced properties will sometimes ask for a reduced commission rate. Instead of 6 percent, perhaps they'll insist on paying no more than 4 percent. (That's still a $40,000 commission on a million dollar property!)

Agents often respond that they are worth the higher commission because they will bring in a higher offer. If that's so, then there is a way to write the listing that gives the agent a sliding scale, a higher commission rate based on a higher selling price, but a lower commission rate based on a lower selling price.

How Much of a Commission Break Might You Get?

Don't expect huge savings when you ask an agent to cut an already agreed-upon commission. Remember, the commission in a typical real estate transaction gets split up many times. In a deal with a 6 percent commission, for example, half may go to the selling office and half to the office representing the buyers. That means that your agent's office gets only 3 percent.

Further, depending on the split arrangement your agent has with his or her office, he or she probably gets half of the half or around 1 $\frac{1}{2}$ percent of the selling price (perhaps a better cut with the office if the agent is a good producer). Thus, out of a $20,000 commission, your agent may actually only be getting $5000.

And, your agent has significant fixed expenses, including car, attire, phone, office, possibly advertising (depending on the arrangement with the office), and so on. Perhaps the fixed expenses come to $2500. That means that the real profit that your agent receives on a $20,000 commission may only be $2500, or less. If the agent splits the profit in half with you, you'd still only likely get $1250. And most agents won't go that far. Thus, you'd probably be lucky to get between $500 and a $1000 from a cooperative agent in our $20,000 commission example.

> Don't expect a big sum of money if the agent agrees to cut the commission. However, any amount is sure to be pleasantly greeted.

Of course, if you negotiate a lower overall commission when you list the property, that's a different story. Your savings there can be far more significant. Reread Chapter 3.

Power Tip 47
Check Your Lender's Payoff
Policy

This is something that too few sellers consider. There may be a significant payoff penalty in your existing mortgage. And there may be ways to avoid it if you're careful.

What Is a Payoff Penalty?

This basically says that if you pay the mortgage off early (any time before it's due, typically in 30 years, or some time before a specific year such as year 5), there's a one-time penalty. The amount of the penalty can vary, but often it is equivalent to 6 months' interest. On a $200,000 mortgage at 8 percent interest, that comes to $8000, a not insignificant chunk of money.

Payoff penalties are both old and new. Back in the 1950s and 1960s, virtually all mortgages had them. The reason they were instituted was to encourage house buyers not to get new financing but, instead, to assume the old existing loans on the property.

Then, when interest rates jumped up in the late 1970s and early 1980s, lenders wanted the opposite. They wanted buyers to dump the old existing loans and get new ones, at higher rates. So they eliminated the prepayment penalty on almost all mortgages and, instead, made the mortgage nonassumable. That meant that the buyer could not take over your existing loan.

More recently, over the past decade when interest rates were falling, lenders were plagued by borrowers who would repeatedly refinance their properties to get ever lower interest rates. To discourage this phenomenon, the prepayment penalty was reinstituted.

However, today's penalty may be different. For example, some prepayment penalties take effect any time you sell your property. Others apply only if you refinance, not if you sell. And others only if you refinance within a certain window, say within 5 years of the time you obtained your loan. (After 5 years, you can sell or refinance with no penalty in this version.)

How Do I Know If I Have a Prepayment Penalty in My Mortgage?

It's not hidden, but it may not have been discussed when you obtained your loan. Or it may have been mentioned, but you didn't pay attention to it or didn't understand it.

The prepayment penalty, if it exists, will be in the loan documents you received when you bought your house. Look for a heading something like one of the following.

Possible Prepayment Headings in Mortgage Documents

- Prepayment of Mortgage Debt
- Early Payoff of Mortgage Balance
- Increase in a Monthly Payment

It could, of course, be under other headings as well.

> You should be aware that the prepayment penalty could cut in if you make an increased monthly payment that goes to principal. Typically, these penalties will apply when the entire mortgage is paid off, but sometimes they also apply if you pay a significant amount, such as 20 percent of the principal, in a single payment. For this reason, you should check your mortgage documents carefully before making a significant principal repayment.

You may also want to call your mortgage lender and ask if your mortgage has a prepayment penalty. However, be prepared not to receive an instant reply.

These days, mortgage servicing changes hands frequently. That means that the lender who originally loaned you the money on your mortgage may no longer hold the debt. Rather, that lender has sold off the "servicing," or collection of the debt, to another company. And that company may have sold it off to yet another, with the process repeated many times. In today's financial marketplace, debt servicing is big business, with large financial institutions trading huge blocks of loans on a fairly regular basis.

All of which is to say that the servicing representative you call on the phone may have no idea if your loan, originally placed with another lender, does or does not have a prepayment penalty. But that person can usually have the mortgage documents researched and come up with an answer, over time. (After all, if you decide to pay off the loan, the servicing company will need to determine if there's a prepayment penalty in order to come up with a payoff amount.) Just be patient. You'll eventually get the word.

How Can I Avoid the Prepayment Penalty?

The bad news may be that your mortgage may, indeed, have a prepayment penalty. The good news is that you may be able to avoid it entirely.

The key to avoiding the prepayment penalty is to see if the lender will choose not to apply it and under what conditions. Most frequently, if you agree to get a new loan with the same lender (or perhaps the current servicing company), the lender may arrange for the prepayment penalty to be voided. The lender may simply carry it forward to the next mortgage. Since, chances are, you're going to buy another house with another mortgage, and assuming the rates are competitive, why not go with your existing lender to save the prepayment penalty?

Less common is the case where if you're a good customer of the lender who holds your mortgage and if you have a lot of money on deposit with the lender, you may be able to pressure the lender to let you avoid the prepayment penalty. (It's usually easier if your lender is a "portfolio lender," or one who does not sell your loan or the servicing of it to another lender. If you got a jumbo loan—a very large mortgage—this may be the case.)

Can I Get the Escrow/Title Insurance Companies Who Handled the Mortgage Originally to Reduce Their Fees?

In addition to getting the mortgage company to void or at least defer the prepayment penalty, you may be able to get the escrow company or the title insurance company or both who handled your mortgage to give you a lower lender's rate. Your leverage is to say you'll deal with them again on your new mortgage (and house purchase), *if* they'll give you a cut-rate deal. See also Tip 41.

Usually, you won't have any trouble getting this if you recently bought the same house through them, say, within the past 2 or 3 years. Because of the reduced paperwork and research involved, they might easily cut your costs by anywhere from 10 to 25 percent.

On the other hand, if you just pressure them by saying you'll only do business with them if they cut you a deal, you might or might not have any luck. A lot will simply depend on how busy they are. If the market is strong, they'll likely pass. On the other hand, if they are handling few houses, they might more seriously consider your offer.

Power Tip 48
Get the Buyer to Pay All or a
Portion of Your Closing Costs

Wouldn't it be nice if the buyers would pick up a portion or even all of your closing costs? It is possible, particularly when the market is hot and there are more buyers than sellers.

Why Would the Buyers Pay Your Costs?

They certainly wouldn't do it out of the generosity of their hearts. However, they might do it if you made it a condition of the sale and if they were desperate to buy your property.

Recently, a friend was selling her house in a tight market. The inventory of available houses for sale was low. And there were many buyers. After a few weeks, she received a full-price offer on her house.

She thought about demanding more than full price, but there weren't multiple offers coming in—she just had the one buyer. And the buyer's agent indicated that this buyer would not pay a dime more in price for the house.

So, my friend countered by putting in a closing-cost contingency. She would accept full price *if* the buyer would agree to pay for all of her nonrecurring (to be explained shortly) closing costs. The buyer eventually agreed and the deal was done.

> Even in more normal markets where price is sometimes a stumbling block, having the buyers pay the sellers' closing costs is a way of increasing the money coming to the sellers, without increasing the price of the house. It works as a tactic when you have a buyer who's hung up about price but is willing to otherwise deal. See also Tip 32 on trading price for terms.

How Is It Handled?

As noted, it should be in the form of a contingency written right into the sales agreement. The sale is made "subject to" the buyers paying all or a portion of the seller's closing costs. A good agent or attorney should be able to write in appropriate language for your deal.

What Are Nonrecurring Closing Costs?

These are one-time costs which are not usually tax deductible. They include the following items.

Nonrecurring Closing Costs

- Title insurance fees
- Escrow charges
- Some fees involved in closing out your mortgage
- Agent's commission
- Other single-charge fees incurred as part of the sale.

What's not usually included in the nonrecurring fees are prorated interest on your mortgage and taxes and sometimes fire insurance.

As you can see, the nonrecurring closing costs can be quite significant. They can add up to many thousands of dollars and can be a real plum if the buyers agree to pay them (or a portion of them).

Why "Nonrecurring?"

"Nonrecurring" is usually found where the seller pays the buyer's costs. Sometimes lenders won't fund a mortgage if someone else is paying the borrower's (buyer's) interest. They want the borrower to pay all recurring costs.

From a seller's perspective, it usually involves tax considerations. Mortgage interest and taxes are normally deductible. But that deduction usually requires two conditions be met: (1) you actually have to pay the interest and taxes and (2) they must be on a debt for which you are liable. If the buyer pays that interest for you, who gets to deduct it? The buyer paid it, so he or she qualifies there. But the debt is in your name in the form of the mortgage, so you qualify there. In the end, no one might be able to deduct it! Hence, prorations of interest and taxes are often also excluded when buyers pay seller's closing costs.

How Is the Payment Handled?

It is normally done in escrow. The costs, instead of appearing on your closing statement, appear on the buyers' closing costs. The buyers, of course, must come up with a considerably greater amount of cash to close the deal.

> The buyers may be able to get the extra cash by increasing the loan to value (LTV) of their financing. For example, if the property is selling for $200,000 and they are getting a standard 80 percent mortgage, they are putting down $40,000. (The mortgage is $160,000). If, however, they instead obtain a 90 percent LTV loan, the mortgage amount jumps up to $180,000 and the cash they need to put down drops to $20,000. That's a $20,000 savings that they can use toward paying your closing costs. (Of course, their monthly payments will be higher.) You might suggest this the next time buyers say they don't have the cash to pay any of your closing costs.

Can I Really Do It?

Negotiating is hard work and you never really can be sure of the outcome in advance. You may decide that a perfectly realistic way of handling the transaction is to have the buyers pay a portion of your closing costs. The market may be strong. And you're sure that the buyers realize that if they don't go along, they'll lose the deal.

However, the buyers may not be willing or able to play ball. Some buyers have a rigid sense of propriety. They may feel that they should pay their costs and you should pay yours. And they are insulted if you ask them to cross the line. To them, it's sort of like stealing.

When you run into buyers who have ethical constraints against paying your costs, don't fight it. Go with the flow. Try to get an equivalent amount by increasing the price accordingly.

On the other hand, sometimes the buyers are simply strapped. They are already at the limit and simply can't come up with any more cash, or can't increase the monthly payments (as would be the case if they increased the LTV as noted earlier). They would like to pay your costs, but don't see how they can do it.

If you don't want to lose this deal and there's no way to get more cash out of the buyers, or to increase the price of the property, consider having the buyers give you a second mortgage or even a promissory note for the closing costs amount. The second mortgage might have a distant due date, with interest, but no monthly payments, so it won't hurt a marginal buyer from qualifying for the loan. When that future date arrives, or the buyer sells the property, you get your money, with interest. A promissory note works the same way, except the property isn't collateral. It's harder to collect in the event the buyer refuses to pay.

Sometimes lenders of a first mortgage won't allow additional secondary financing, particularly if the buyer is weak. In this case, you won't be able to use a second mortgage. But a promissory note probably would still work.

Keep in mind that there are all kinds of creative solutions for increasing your revenue from the sale. And having the buyers pay your closing costs is just one of them.

11
Save More on Taxes

Power Tip 49
Take the Up-to-$250,000
Exclusion

The tax law is somewhat strange when it comes to selling your property. If you have a gain (a profit), you will be taxed on it. On the
other hand, if you have a loss (and the property is your principal residence), you can't deduct the loss! Of course, it tends to come out
in the wash since, in most cases, even if you have a gain, you won't
need to worry about paying taxes on it because of the huge exclusion on principal residences that the government allows.

> The purpose of this tip is to give an overview of how taxation
> can affect the sale of property, not to provide specific informa-
> tion on how to handle your taxes. For tax help, consult with a
> tax professional.

What Is a Gain?

While it seems easy to say that a taxing gain is the same as a profit,
that's not always the case: it could be more or less. The government
calculates gain in a very specific way. Generally speaking, you figure
your gain on the sale of your house by subtracting your tax basis
from your sale price. The calculation looks something like this:

Calculating Gain

Price realized (less costs of sale)	$200,000
Less adjusted tax basis	150,000
Taxable gain	$ 50,000

> The tax basis is generally what you paid for the property. From
> it you *add* costs of purchase and *add* any improvements (such
> as an addition). This is called the "adjusted" basis.

On the property just mentioned, the gain would be $50,000.
That's the amount on which you would owe taxes..

What Is the Exclusion?

However, you probably won't have to pay any tax on the gain. The government allows you to exclude up to $250,000 for a single person or up to $500,000 for a married couple. Since in the preceding example the amount is far less than either of these figures, there is no tax to be paid.

> You must qualify for the exclusion. The two major qualifications are that: (1) the house must be your principal residence and (2) you must have lived in it for the previous 2 out of the previous 5 years.

What Is a Principal Residence?

The definition is sufficiently broad to include a lot of different types of property. Basically, a *principal residence* is where you live most of the time, your main house. It can include any of the following.

Typical Principal Residences

- A single-family house
- A condo or a coop
- One unit of a duplex, triplex, or bigger multiple-dwelling property
- A houseboat
- A motor home

   Chances are the property you're selling, if you live there most of the time, will qualify as a principal residence.

What Is "2 Out of 5" Years?

Counting back from the date of sale, you have 5 years in which you must have lived 2 of them on the property in order to qualify. If you've lived there for the past 5 years continuously, then you've got no problem.

   You don't have to have lived there continuously. You might have lived there for the last year, but rented the property out for 3 years, prior to which you lived there. Again, if it's 2 out of the previous 5, you qualify.

On the other hand, if, for example, you only lived there 18 months out of the previous 5 years, then you probably would not qualify. If you don't qualify, then you'll have to pay tax on your gain.

What If There Were Extenuating Circumstances?

If, for example, you had to sell the property after only 1 year because of a job change or because of health reasons, you might qualify for a portion of the exclusion. (If you lived there 12 out of the required 24 months, you'd probably get half the exclusion.)

Remember, however, this is *only* if there are qualifying extenuating circumstances. Be sure to check with your tax advisor here.

What If I'm Single?

You don't have to be married to get the exclusion. Quite the opposite. It is written specifically for individuals. It is a $250,000-per-person exclusion, which married couples, may double up to reach $500,000. Single is okay, here.

How Often Can I Use the Exclusion?

Since the property must be your principal residence and since you must live there for at least 2 years, you can only use the exclusion once every 2 years.

What About Replacing the House and Deferring the Gain?

Those were the old rules prior to the 1997 Tax Act, which changed the tax code. You may have heard of these because they were used so often by house owners. In the old days, the gain was not excluded (meaning you would eventually have to pay it). It was deferred into the future by subtracting it from the basis of your next property. And you generally had only 2 years to replace your existing house. Under the current rules, you can take the money and run. You're not required to replace your current house.

What about the Once in a Lifetime Exclusion?

Another old rule. Prior to 1997, if you reached the age of 55 (and otherwise qualified), you could exclude up to $125,000 of your gain on the sale of your principal residence. That's no longer the case. Remember, now you can exclude up to $250,000 per person. There is no limit on age or on how many times you use the exclusion.

Is the Exclusion Automatic?

When you sell your house, bring your sales documents to your accountant. He or she can handle it for you. There is no specific form to fill out.

Is the Money Mine to Do with As I Want?

As noted earlier, you can use it on a vacation, to purchase another house, to help with your child's education, even to gamble away at a casino. There is no restriction on how you spend it. You are not required to reinvest any of it in another house, although you probably would be wise to do so given the way property values are going up.

Power Tip 50
Take the Home Office
Deduction Sparingly

You should take the home office deduction if it happens to make financial sense for you. For many people, however, the new rules make it unadvisable to take this deduction.

> The purpose of this tip is to give an overview of how taxation can affect the sale of property, not to provide specific information on how to handle your taxes. For tax help, consult with a tax professional.

What Is the Home Office Deduction?

Many people operate a business out of their houses. If you don't, then this tip probably won't help you very much. But if you do, read on.

The government, in a variety of tax code changes, has liberalized the home office deduction. Indeed, if you qualify, the government encourages you to take it.

Basically, the home office deduction allows you to deduct from your taxes the cost of operating an office out of your house. Besides the usual business expenses such as phone, advertising, secretarial work, and so on, this means that you can deduct a portion of your house expenses from your annual income taxes.

For example, you may be able to deduct a portion of what you annually pay for:

- Mortgage interest
- Property taxes
- Insurance
- Utilities

In addition, you may be able to depreciate that portion of the house which you deduct for business use. For some people with a large home business, the deduction can be substantial.

The depreciation deduction is a great incentive. It allows you deduct *more* than you actually spend. All of the other expenses are dollar for dollar. Depreciation, however, is in a sense imaginary dollars. It's the loss of value of the property over time. You don't actually spend it out of your pocket (indeed, most properties go up in value), yet you still get to take the deduction.

Who Qualifies to Take the Deduction?

The rules have been liberalized so more people who operate home businesses can take the deduction. Generally speaking, you must operate a successful business, that is, your business must make money.

> If you have a business which loses money every year, the Internal Revenue Service may declare it not a real business but a hobby instead. You can't take deductions for a hobby.

You must also use your house regularly for your business activities. In the past this eliminated many salespeople and others who conducted a large portion of their business activities on the road. Under more recent rulings, as long as a substantial portion of your business is conducted at home, you may be able to take the home office deduction.

Does the House Have to Qualify?

Not the house, but the office. The area used for your home office cannot be used for any other activity. In other words, you cannot use a bedroom part time as your office and part time as a guest bedroom (where people sleep). Any usage as a bedroom denies usage as an office. It must be exclusively used as your home office 100 percent of the time.

The calculation of how much of your house qualifies as the office is made on the basis of the square footage used. For example, if you have a 2000-square-foot house and you are using a 200 square-foot bedroom exclusively and fully as your home office, 10 percent of your house is the office.

What this means is that when you take your deduction, you would, for example, deduct 10 percent of your mortgage interest. And 10 percent of your property taxes. And you make the calculation for depreciation on your entire house and then take 10 percent of it to deduct for your home office.

While 10 percent may turn out to be a fairly small amount, some people with home business use a much larger portion of their house for this activity. Imagine, for example, how large the deduction would be if 50 percent of your house were used for a home office.

What's the Problem with Taking a Home Office Deduction?

In order to see the problem, let's compare how a home office deduction was handled in the past when you sold your house with how it's handled now.

In The Past Before the current rules, if you had an office in your house when you sold your property, you were required to pay capital gains tax on the gain on that business portion. This could prove to be a hardship since if you were "rolling the property over," that is taking advantage of the old deferral rules noted in Tip 49, you deferred paying tax on the rest of the property, but not on the home office portion. In our earlier example, you would have to pay capital gains tax on 10 percent of the gain of your house, while deferring it on 90 percent, instead of being able to defer it on 100 percent. Having a business use kicked in the capital gains tax.

Currently Things are a bit different today. Today you are required to recapture the amount you deducted for depreciation and some other expenses from your home office when you sell your house. In other words, It's not simply a matter of paying the capital gains tax on the office portion. If you used it for 10 years, when you sell, you have 10 years of recapture to pay taxes on!

Further, the amount recaptured may be at a rate higher than the normal capital gains tax rate. (The recapture rate is scheduled to change. Check with your accountant for the exact rate.)

Thus, when you sell currently, while you may be able to exclude all of your gain (up to the $250,000 limitations noted earlier) on the personal use portion of your house, you'll have to recapture your previous deductions going back through the years and then pay a relatively stiff tax rate on it. The taxes, even when you're only deducting 10 percent of the area of your house, can be significant at the time of sale.

Is It Worth It?

Of course, you got the deduction all those years on your income taxes. And, depending on your tax bracket, that annual deduction may more than offset the tax you'll pay on gains when you sell.

The only way to know for sure is to have your accountant calculate it both ways for you. You may find that it makes more sense for you *not* to take home office deduction. Or, it could go the other way.

12

Sell Quickly in Any Market

Power Tip 51
Try Auctioning Off Your House

A real estate auction is like any other kind of auction—from rare paintings to automobiles. Essentially, you sell your house off to the highest bidder. In both hot markets and cold, an auction, if cleverly done, can sometimes produce the highest price in the quickest way for your house.

How Is It Done?

Although it can take far longer in preparation, the easiest way to think of a house auction is to break it down into a single week. Here are the components.

A Week to Auction Your House

Day 1. Print up brochures and billboards and be sure to place an advertisement in the local newspaper (placed the previous week before the paper's deadline).

Days 2-6. Get the word out that you're having an auction. Put billboards up around area, particularly where people drive by such as on heavily trafficked streets. Be sure you get permission for the billboards—some communities have stiff fines for placement without a license. Have your house open for viewing.

Day 7—morning. Get bidders to sign in and show their preapproval letters (described later in this chapter). Have the property open for inspection.

Day 7—early afternoon. Have the auction. Check with the auctioneer for exact timing.

Day 7—late afternoon. Have the winning bidder sign the sales agreement and open escrow.

Promoting the Auction

The key to any auction is getting a lot of qualified bidders to attend. That's up to you. Here are some ways to get publicity.

Publicizing Your Auction

- Advertise on your public access channel if your cable company has one.
- Advertise in the local newspaper.
- Put up billboards.
- Hand out brochures at all local real estate offices.
- Hang brochures in local supermarkets, where possible.
- Pass brochures out at housing offices of local corporations.

The idea is to make as many people as possible aware of your auction.

Generate Excitement

Bidders will attend, *if* they think there's an opportunity for them. In a hot market, they'll come because it's a chance to get a house, any house, when the inventory is small and there are too many buyers.

In a normal to cold market, they'll come because they hope to get a bargain—a house selling for less than market price.

Your advertising (newspaper, brochure, billboard, and so on) must generate excitement. Phrases such as, "Local House to Be Auctioned Off to Highest Bidder!" will help. "Bidding Open to Everyone.*" The asterisk leads to a statement that all bidders must have a preapproval letter from a lender. "Chance of a lifetime!" and other puffery also can be useful.

> A preapproval letter means the potential buyer has filled out a loan application, the lender has conducted at minimum a credit check, and, as a result, the lender makes a statement that it's willing to loan up to a certain amount to this person. It's your assurance that you're dealing with a person who actually can afford to purchase the house.

Get Bidders to Sign In

You should get all bidders to sign in, at least at the time of the auction, if not sooner. It's a good idea to have them, in addition to the preapproval letter, pay a fully refundable deposit in order to bid. Ideally, the amount should be $1000, or more, to be applied to the winning bid and returned to everyone else. However, as a practical matter, the amount can be only $100 or even as little as $25. The idea is to keep frivolous bids out.

At the time of sign-in, you should give the bidders the terms of the auction. Usually, these include the fact that the successful bidder must put up a deposit of $5000 (or whatever amount you feel appropriate to cement the deal) immediately after winning and sign a sales agreement. The terms of the sales agreement should also be spelled out. They may include an inspection report contingency, as well as a financing contingency, to protect the buyer should he or she not be able to get a loan. You can also hand out (and have bidders sign for) a disclosure statement at the time they sign up for the auction.

Typically, you will assign bidders a number. You may even hand out little flags with their numbers on it so they can raise the flag to indicate their bid.

Have the Auctioneer Conduct the Auction

If you're going to be successful, you need to hire a professional auctioneer. If you've ever been to a real auction, you'll know why without me telling you. A professional auctioneer gets the crowd aroused and enthusiastic. He or she gets people to bid who would normally never raise their hands. The auctioneer starts bidding wars between bidders. In short, without a professional auctioneer, your chances of successfully pulling it off are virtually zip.

The professional auctioneer can give you many tips on how to conduct the auction and how to get more bidders in. A professional auctioneer will cost you money, often as much as $1000 or more. But don't scrimp here. The professional auctioneer will more than earn his or her fee back by getting you a higher price.

You can find an auctioneer simply by checking in the phone book under "auctions." If possible, try to get one who belongs to the National Association of Auctioneers.

One of the big problems of a single house auction is that there is no buildup. With only one item to sell, there's no chance for the auctioneer to get the crowd excited. Everything happens too fast. Therefore, it's useful to slow the auction down by selling half a dozen or more items early on. Why not sell your appliances, furniture, even clothing? It can be a glorified yard sale. And with these, if they go for bargain prices, it will only peak the crowd's interest in the final item, the house.

What If the House Sells for Less Than Market?

This, of course, is a realistic fear. What if there are few bidders? What if those who are there don't bid high enough? You could end up selling your house for less than it's worth!

It's important to understand that there are two kinds of auction. One has a reserve; the other is absolute (without reserve). In a reserve auction, you reserve the right to refuse sale unless the winning bid is above a predetermined price. For example, your reserve might be $180,000. If no bid comes in at or above that amount, you don't have to go through with the sale. In an absolute auction, the property goes to the highest bidder, no matter how low that bid may be.

In most states you are legally required to tell bidders if it is a reserve auction. Some states may require you to use a licensed auctioneer.

You will generate far more interest in your auction if it is absolute, without reserve. Although this is riskier, it indicates to bidders that they could get a real bargain; hence, more will tend to come out. You must be a real gambler to feel comfortable with an absolute auction.

What about Working with Agents?

There is no reason an auction should eliminate agents. Indeed, you want them to work with you. You can advertise that you'll pay a buyer's commission (typically 3 percent) to any agent who brings in a successful bidder.

Of course, the agent must sign the bidder in. This protects you against agents claiming a commission later on for someone whom they may not have been working with directly.

Check Out Local Regulations

Some states regulate auctions. If you hire a professional auctioneer, he or she should be able to tell you about any rules or licensing by which you must abide.

Where Should the Auction Be Held?

It needs to be in an area large enough to accommodate all of those attending. It also should be near the house so bidders can inspect the property.

Often the back or front yard will do nicely. Be sure there are chairs for people to sit on. And if it's sunny, you may want to provide large umbrellas. Professional auctions are often conducted in rented tents.

> You may want to pass out champagne to adult bidders, provided this does not violate alcohol regulations in your state. It adds to the pageantry, gets people in the mood, and can loosen wallets so they'll bid higher!

Power Tip 52
Consider a "Short Sale"

A *short sale* is used when you're "upside down" on your house. This means that you owe more than your house is worth. The short sale means that the lender accepts less than the amount owed (a short payoff), which allows you to conclude the sale. It's one way out of a difficult situation.

Short Sale in a Hot Market

Short sales in hot markets normally only occur when owners have borrowed more than their house is worth. For example, if you took out one of the 125 percent mortgages that are readily available these days and were forced to sell before your house went up in value, you would owe more than your house is worth. (Illness, job loss or change, or any of a large number of other factors could force you to sell sooner than you expected.) For example, your loan might be $250,000 and your house might only be worth $200,000.

Some borrowers think they can simply walk away from this debt. However, besides ruining your credit, walking away might not be a solution. You could be personally liable for the difference between what the house brings and the loan amount.

One-hundred-twenty-five-percent loans come in two flavors. In one, the property is the entire collateral. However, if you just walk away, the lender may be able to choose a judicial foreclosure (even if the debt is evidenced by a trust deed), which means that a deficiency judgment could be obtained against you—you would then be personally liable for the loss the lender sustains and the debt would follow you wherever you went.

In the second variety, the loan is part personal and part real estate. Here, you're liable for the debt immediately if you fail to make your payments and the lender calls in the loan.

Short Sale in a Normal to Cold Market

In a more normal or even a cold market, property values haven't gone up or might even have gone down. Again, you owe more than your house is worth.

For example, you might have obtained near 100 percent financing. But the market is stagnant, and your house is only worth what you paid for it. The trouble is the transaction costs. With agent's fees and closing costs, it can cost you 10 percent of its value to sell it. You might have paid $150,000 for your house, which is what your mortgage is for. But it will cost you $15,000 in agent's fees and other costs to sell it. So, you're upside down by that amount of money.

In a cold market, you might have put down 20 percent, but your house's value has fallen 25 percent. Add in transaction costs and you're very much upside down.

Getting a Short Sale

One way out of all of these problem situations is to get the lender to accept less. If the lender accepts less than it is owed, you can sell your house and get out from under. Getting the lender to this, however, is the trick.

You must approach the lender and apprise it of the problem. Don't think the lender knows what the situation is. Explain it.

> Chances are you'll be having trouble making payments and one of the lender's credit people will be calling to see what's wrong. Explain the house's situation. Ask right out if the lender will accept a short sale.

Expect the lender's initial reaction to be negative. The lender may simply refuse to consider a short sale out of hand. The reason is that the lender wants all of its money back. Anything less than all represents a loss, and lenders aren't in business to lose money.

Further, the lender always hopes (and will tell you this) that to preserve your credit, you will continue making those loan payments until you're in your grave. Expect stiff lectures on the importance of good credit and how failing to maintain your payments will ruin your credit. If the lender can bully you into continuing to make payments, it probably will.

All of this means that you must convince the lender that you're serious about having to dump the property. One person I knew in this situation simply stopped making payments. Within 3 months, the lender was convinced it had to find another way out, and considered a short sale. Yes, the missed payments did adversely affect the borrowers credit, but not nearly as much as a foreclosure would have.

The lender also must be convinced that the house cannot be sold for enough to clear the loan. If the lender thinks the house can be sold for enough, it will be simply pursue foreclosure, take the property back, and resell it itself.

> A bank near where I live is currently offering a house for sale at $240,000. It foreclosed at $220,000, waited a short while until the market went up, and is now planning to resell the house at a profit. Don't expect the lender to go for a short sale if it sees another way to get its money out, let alone make a profit.

Find a Buyer

Once the bank gives some indication that it might accept a short payoff and short sale (no matter how slight it might be), find a buyer. You may need to sell the property yourself because you won't have the cash to pay an agent. Do it. (See earlier tips on selling your house yourself.)

When you find a buyer, get a sales agreement signed, making it contingent upon the lender accepting a short sale. Then, take the sales agreement to the lender and point out the obvious.

1. You have to move and can't afford to keep making the payments.

2. You have a buyer in hand.

3. Either the lender accepts the buyer's offer, including a short sale, or it will have to take the property back through foreclosure.

Depending on the market strength, the lender's disposition (a few lenders will not accept a short sale no matter what and there's no reasoning with them), and how good the offer is, you might just get the lender to accept a short payoff and a short sale.

It's more likely a lender will accept a short payoff/short sale in a normal to cold market, with prices flat or declining. In a hot market, the lender may simply prefer to foreclose and take its chances at reselling the house at a profit, as noted earlier.

Have the Mortgage Switched to Another Property

An alternative to a short sale is to have the "too big" mortgage switched to another property by the lender. You sell this property for what you can get, and then you have the full remaining balance of the mortgage switched to a new property that you buy.

Some lenders will go along with this; some won't. The biggest stumbling block is usually finding a second property that will appraise for enough to accommodate the bigger mortgage and that you can still afford.

Beware of Tax Consequences

If you have a short sale and a short payoff, you may think you're home free. Think again. The IRS could go after you for the profit you made on the sale!

What profit, you may be asking? You sold for a loss.

Yes, but according to IRS rules, if debt is forgiven, as is the case in a short sale/short payoff, that forgiven debt is considered income. Thus, if you owe $145,000 and your lender accepts a short payoff of $125,000, you may end up having to declare $20,000 as income on which you would need to pay taxes!

Be sure to check with your accountant about the tax consequences before accepting a short sale. New laws are pending in Congress as of this writing to do away with this absurd penalty.

Power Tip 53
Offer a Lease Option

If you're having trouble selling your property to buyers, consider selling it to tenants. Many tenants would love to purchase the house they are renting, except they don't have the cash for the down payment. The lease option may offer them the opportunity and, in the process, get rid of your property.

Rent Instead of Sell

An age-old option for anyone who can't sell his or her house is to rent it out. At least if you rent out the property, you can get money in to help make the mortgage and tax payment.

However, renting your house carries with it certain headaches. You become a landlord. That means you can be called at all times of the day or night to fix anything that goes wrong from a leaky faucet to a broken window.

Further, tenants may not take as good care of your property as you did. Thus, when the current tenants finally move out, you may need to refurbish the place either to rerent it or to try and sell it again.

How Does the Lease Option Work?

One way out of this quagmire is to use a lease option instead of a standard rental agreement. A lease option converts your tenant into a potential buyer who will usually take better care of the property (since they'll soon own it).

A lease option works in a simple way. You have a standard lease; however, it's usually for 2 or 3 years instead of the usual 6 months to 1 year.

In addition, you give the tenant the written option to buy your property at the end of the lease. Normally, the purchase price is written in. (There may or may not be a separate option price or fee.)

Further, you grant the tenant that a portion of each month's rent will go toward the down payment. This is the key to the success or failure of the lease option.

For example, a tenant may be paying $1000 a month. Under a conventional lease, you get all of that money; the tenant never sees it again.

Under the lease option, a portion of it, say $500, goes toward the down payment when the tenant purchases the house. At the end of 2 years, the tenant would have accumulated a down payment credit of $12,000 and $18,000 after 3 years.

When the tenant exercises the option, you credit the tenant with whatever amount was determined to go toward the down payment. In some cases it may be the entire down payment, in others a significant portion.

Additionally, the tenant often pays more than market rent. For example, if your house would normally rent out for $850, under a lease option you may rent it out for $1000. The tenant is willing to pay extra because a significant portion of the rent is going toward a future down payment.

What Makes a Lease Option Successful?

As noted, the key to success in a lease option is the amount of the tenant's rent that goes toward the eventual down payment. It must be large enough to offer a realistic hope of turning into a true down payment. If it's too small, the tenant will begin to see that he or she will never really accumulate enough for the down payment, will begin to resent paying a higher rental rate, and may take that resentment out by harming the property, walking away, or both.

The biggest mistake that owner's make is to try to take too much of the monthly payment for themselves. If, when you begin the lease option, you think only about all that rent money you'll lose because it's going to the tenant's down payment and, therefore, reduce the amount that is applied to the down payment, you're breeding the seeds of a failed contract. Yes, you might get the tenant to pay for a while, but eventually the tenant may do harm to your property, not to mention simply walking away.

> Give the tenant a big chunk of the monthly payment and you'll help ensure loyalty and an eventual sale. And, after all, selling is your goal.

How Do I Get It Drawn Up?

Generic lease-option documents are available in stationery stores and over the Internet at various sites. However, if you're serious about doing this, I would have an attorney draw up a document specific to your needs. Yes, it will cost you a couple of hundred bucks, but in the long run it should save you a lot of hassle and headache.

How Do I Qualify the Tenant?

Not every tenant wants to buy the house they are living in. And even of those that do, not everyone will be able to accomplish the task. Remember, in addition to the down payment, there's the mortgage that the tenant will need to get to complete the sale.

Therefore, you must be very careful when soliciting tenants and should screen them closely. In addition to the usual things you look for in any tenant (good credit history, recommendations from previous landlords, the ability to come up with both the first month's rent and a hefty security deposit, and so on), you may also require the tenant to get a preapproval letter from a lender.

You'll recall that a preapproval letter is obtained when a borrower fills out a loan application and the lender secures a credit report. It states the maximum amount of mortgage (or maximum monthly) payment that the borrower can afford.

When tenants get a preapproval letter, you can see whether or not they can qualify to purchase your house. Of course, the letter is for now and the actual purchase will take place several years into the future. Things change and your tenants may end up with a worse, or better, financial situation. Nevertheless, it at least helps to ensure that initially they could qualify to purchase your house.

What Can Go Wrong with a Lease Option?

Lots. My own experience with these has not always been satisfactory. Here are a few of the problems that can arise.

Problems with a Lease Option

- The tenants discover, after living there for a while, that they don't like it and decide they don't want to buy it. Now they resent the higher rent they are paying and want to leave before the end of the lease.

- The market changes and mortgage interest rates rise, meaning that the tenants can't qualify to buy the house at the end of the term. You're still stuck with the property.

- The tenants hit a financial bad spot and can't keep making the high monthly payments. You eventually have to evict them.

- The tenants stop making payments, move out, and leave the property a mess, requiring you to spend money out of your pocket to fix it up.

- Property values rise and by the time the tenants exercise their option, you're locked into selling the house at below market! (You can include an inflation clause in the option that will help overcome this problem—check with the attorney who draws it up.)

- You have the property listed and the broker only wants a sale and a commission. (In actual practice, the reason for the lease option is that you can't sell.)

> If you can't sell the property, most agents will go along with a lease option. They will usually be willing to handle the lease option paperwork for you, accepting a small fee (perhaps 1 month's rent) or no commission, provided they get their full commission later on when the tenants exercise their option to buy.

Of course, you might have a perfectly successful lease-option experience. But then, again, you might not. It's important to see this as one alternative but not as a panacea.

Power Tip 54
Sell "As Is"

"As is" means without fixing anything. Normally, when you sell a house, there is an implied warranty that says you are offering the house in good condition. The buyer gets a house inspection and disclosures and if there are any defects, you either fix them out of hand or you negotiate over getting them fixed.

Not so with an "as is" sale. Here, no matter what is disclosed or discovered, you won't fix it. You're selling the house as it stands, defects and all.

What's the Advantage of Selling "As Is"?

There are several advantages, as well as several problems, with selling your house this way. The two biggest plusses are the following.

Plusses for Selling "As Is"

1. *You obviously don't have to do any work fixing up the property.* This can be a big headache removed if the house has a serious problem such as a bad roof or a cracked foundation. Even if the problems are only minor, you don't have to worry about them.

2. *You may get a quicker sale.* Buyers are always looking for bargains and "as is" houses are considered bargain properties. Therefore, as soon as you put your house up for sale "as is," expect the volume of buyers to increase dramatically.

What's the Downside of Selling "As Is?"

On the other hand, there is a big negative with selling "as is."

Negative with Selling "As Is" You'll probably get less for your house. As noted earlier, buyers are looking for a bargain with an "as is" house because they figure there must be something wrong with it (why else would you sell this way). Hence, you can expect lots of lowball offers, with the result that you'll probably end up selling for a lower price.

I recently bought a house that was advertised "as is." The reason it was being sold in this fashion was that it was owned by a relocation company that simply didn't want to be bothered with doing any fix-up work. (Additionally, the relocation company got its fee regardless of the selling price—any loss was picked up by the corporation which had hired it and which had transferred a worker.)

The relocation company/sellers wanted a quick sale. And they got one, within 2 weeks. However, they also had to accept a price that was below market.

Fix Up the House

If you want top dollar for your property, fix it up. As described in Chapter 5, a dressed-up property will attract buyers who will be more inclined to pay a higher price.

Sometimes sellers with a distressed house (or a house that's distressing) don't have the money on hand to do the fixup. If you're in that situation, I suggest you consider a home equity loan. They can be obtained almost overnight and should be for enough to fix most problems. Alternatively, credit cards can be used for short-term debt to pay for a fixup.

On the other hand, if you don't want to bother with fixup, if you don't have time, or if you just want to get out fast, sell "as is."

Do I Still Have to Give Disclosures to the Buyers?

Indeed you do, either because it's required in your state or because the buyers make it a condition of purchase. It's important to understand that selling "as is" doesn't mean hiding anything from the buyers. Indeed, you want even more disclosure than selling it fixed up!

The reason is that you don't want buyers coming back after the sale, claiming foul because there was a hidden defect. You can scream that you sold the property "as is," defects and all. But the buyers will surely say that the price they paid was based on the house with the defects that were disclosed; they would have offered less or wouldn't have bought if they had known about the hidden defect. They may even say that you purposely hid a defect which you knew about, hoping to avoid a problem by selling "as is."

For this reason, I strongly suggest disclosing any and all defects to buyers, especially when selling "as is."

How Can I Get a Better Price Selling "As Is"?

Selling "as is" doesn't mean you can't do any fixup work; you can. You can do all the sorts of cosmetic things that help make a house show well. You can paint the inside and outside, work on the land-scaping, put in new carpeting, and so on. You can dress the place up to look like a dollhouse, and then still sell "as is."

Why would you want to? Because there might be a serious defect in the property.

I was recently looking at a house that was fixed up in this way. It really looked terrific, ready to move in. I could see why a buyer would definitely find it appealing. But since the seller was offering it "as is," I asked why?

The candid reply was that the house was on a slipping foundation. It had already slid nearly half a foot down a hillside, and it could slip farther. The sellers brought out detailed rescue plans produced by a builder who said it could be fixed for around $75,000. The price had been adjusted accordingly

The sellers weren't hiding the problem; indeed, they made a point of telling buyers about it. However, because the house looked so appealing, buyers who would otherwise never consider a house with such a serious problem were actually making offers. The house sold within 3 weeks.

By the way, I also asked the sellers why they didn't pop for the $75,000 and fix the problem themselves. They replied because there was no guarantee the fix would work. And they didn't want to be responsible for it after the sale. If they sold "as is," the buyers would be responsible for fixing up the property. If the fix didn't work, then it would be their headache.

Selling "as is" can be a useful tool for drawing buyers and quickly getting rid of a house with problems. By fixing it up, you can even hope to get quicker sale.

Appendix

Terms You Need to Understand

If you're just getting introduced to real estate, you'll quickly realize that people in this field speak a different language. There are "points" and "disclosures" and "contingencies" and dozens of other terms that can make you think people are talking in a foreign language.

While this should be a tiny stumbling block that can be quickly overcome with occasionally humorous results (over terms you don't understand), too often the real consequences are that you get confused and perhaps even act (or fail to act) on something important. Therefore, it's a good idea to become familiar with the following terms, which are frequently used in real estate.

Abstract of Title: A written document produced by a title insurance company (in some states an attorney will do it) giving the history of who owned the property from the first owner forward. It also indicates any liens or encumbrances that may affect the title. A lender will not make a loan, nor can a sale normally conclude, until the title to real estate is clear as evidenced by the abstract.

Acceleration Clause: A clause that "accelerates" the payments in a mortgage, meaning that the entire amount becomes immediately due and payable. Most mortgages contain this clause (which kicks in if, for example, you sell the property).

Adjustable Rate Mortgage (ARM): A mortgage whose interest rate fluctuates according to an index and a margin agreed to in advance by borrower and lender.

Adjustment Date: The day on which an adjustment is made in an adjustable rate mortgage. It may occur monthly, every six months, once a year, or as otherwise agreed.

Agent: Any person licensed to sell real estate, whether a broker or a salesperson.

Alienation Clause: A clause in a mortgage specifying that if the property is transferred to another person, the mortgage becomes immediately due and payable. (See also **Acceleration Clause.**)

ALTA: American Land Title Association. A more complete and extensive policy of title insurance and one that most lenders insist upon. It involves a physical inspection and often guarantees the property's boundaries. Lenders often insist on an ALTA policy, with themselves named as beneficiary.

Amortization: Paying back the mortgage in equal installments. In other words, if the mortgage is for 30 years, you pay in 360 equal installments. (The last payment is often a few dollars more or less. This is opposed to a **Balloon Payment,** which is considerably larger than the rest.

Annual Percentage Rate (APR): The rate paid for a loan, including interest, loan fees, and points. As determined by a government formula.

Appraisal: Evaluation of a property usually by a qualified appraiser, as required by most lenders. The amount of the appraisal is the maximum value on which the loan will be based. For example, if the appraisal is $100,000 and the lender loans 80 percent of value, the maximum mortgage will be $80,000.

ASA: American Society of Appraisers. A professional organization of appraisers.

As Is: A property sold without warrantees from the sellers. The sellers are essentially saying that they won't make any repairs.

Assignment of Mortgage: The lender's sale of a mortgage usually without the borrower's permission. For example, you may obtain a mortgage from XYZ Savings and Loan, which then sells the mortgage to Bland Bank. You will get a letter saying that the mortgage was assigned and you are to make your payments to a new entity. The document used between lenders for the transfer is the "assignment of mortgage."

Assumption: Taking over an existing mortgage. For example, a seller may have an assumable mortgage on a property. When you buy the property, you take over that seller's obligation under the loan. Today most fixed rate mortgages are not assumable. Most adjustable rate mortgages are, but the borrower must qualify. FHA and VA mortgages may be assumable if certain conditions are met. When you assume the mortgage, you may be personally liable if there is a foreclosure.

Automatic Guarantee: The power assigned to some lenders to guarantee VA loans without first checking with the Veterans Administration. These lenders can often make the loans more quickly.

Backup: An offer that comes in after an earlier offer is accepted. If both buyer and seller agree, the backup assumes a secondary position to be acted upon only if the original deal does not go through.

Balloon Payment: A single mortgage payment, usually the last, that is larger than all the others. In the case of second mortgages held by sellers, often only interest is paid until the due date—then the entire amount borrowed (the principal) is due. (See **Second Mortgage.**)

Biweekly Mortgage: A mortgage that is paid every other week instead of monthly. Since there are 52 weeks in the year, you end up making 26 payments, or the equivalent of one month's extra payment. The additional payments, applied to principal, significantly reduce the amount of interest charged on the mortgage and often reduce the term of the loan.

Blanket Mortgage: One mortgage that covers several properties instead of a single mortgage on each property. It is used most frequently by developers and builders.

Broker: An independent licensed agent, one who can establish his or her own office. Salespeople must work for brokers, typically for a few years, to get enough experience to become licensed as brokers.

Buy-Down Mortgage: A mortgage with a lower than market interest rate, either for the entire term of the mortgage or for a set period at the beginning—say, 2 years. The buy-down is made possible by the builder or seller paying an up-front fee to the lender.

Buyer's Agent: A real estate agent whose loyalty is to the buyer and not to the seller. Such agents are becoming increasingly common today.

Call Provision: A clause in a mortgage allowing the lender to call in the entire unpaid balance of the loan providing certain events have occurred, such as sale of the property. (See also **Acceleration Clause.**)

Canvass: To work a neighborhood, to go through it and knock on every door. Agents canvas to find listings. Investors and home buyers do it to find potential sellers who have not yet listed their property—and may agree to sell quickly for less.

Caps: Limits put on an adjustable rate mortgage. The interest rate, the monthly payment, or both may be capped.

Certificate of Reasonable Value (CRV): A document issued by the Veterans Administration establishing what the VA feels is the property's maximum value. In some cases, if a buyer pays more than this amount for the property, he or she will not qualify for the VA loan.

Chain of Title: The history of ownership of the property. The title to property forms a chain going back to the first owners, which in the Southwest, for example, may come from original Spanish land grants.

Closing: When the seller conveys title to the buyer and the buyer makes full payment, including financing, for the property. At the closing, all required documents are signed and delivered and funds are disbursed.

Commission: The fee charged for an agent's services. Usually, but not always, the seller pays. There is no "set" fee; rather, the amount is fully negotiable.

Commitment: A written promise from lender to borrower offering a mortgage at a set amount, interest rate, and cost. Typically, commitments have a time limit—for example, they are good for 30 days or 45 days. Some lenders charge for making a commitment if you don't subsequently take out the mortgage (since they have tied up the money for that amount of time). When the lender's offer is in writing, it is sometimes called a "firm commitment."

Conforming Loan: A mortgage that conforms to the underwriting requirements of Fannie Mae and Freddie Mac.

Construction Loan: A mortgage made for the purpose of constructing a building. The loan is short term, typically under 12 months, and is usually paid in installments directly to the builder as the work is completed. Most often, it is interest only.

Contingency: A condition that limits a contract. For example, the most common contingency says that a buyer is not required to complete a purchase if he or she fails to get necessary financing. (See also **Subject To.**)

Conventional Loan: Any loan that is not guaranteed or insured by the government.

Convertible Mortgage: An adjustable rate mortgage (ARM) with a clause allowing it to be converted to a fixed rate mortgage at some time in the future. You may have to pay an additional cost to obtain this type of mortgage.

Cosigner: Someone with better credit (usually a close relative) who agrees to sign your loan if you do not have good enough credit to qualify for a mortgage. The cosigner is equally responsible for repayment of the loan. (Even if you don't pay it back, the cosigner can be held liable for the entire balance.)

Credit Report: A report, usually from one of the country's three large credit reporting companies, that gives your credit history. It typically lists all your delinquent payments or failures to pay as well as any bankruptcies and, sometimes, foreclosures. Lenders use the report to determine whether to offer you a mortgage. The fee for obtaining the report is usually under $50, and you are charged for it.

Deal Point: Any point on which the deal hinges. It can be as important as the price or as trivial as changing the color of the mailbox.

Deposit: The money that buyers put up (also called "earnest money") to demonstrate their seriousness in making an offer. The deposit is usually at risk if the buyers fail to complete the transaction and have no acceptable way of backing out of the deal.

Disclosures: A list and explanation of features and defects in a property that sellers give to buyers. Most states now require disclosures.

Discount: The amount that a lender withholds from a mortgage to cover the points and fees. For example, you may borrow $100,000, but your points and fees come to $3,000; hence the lender will fund only $97,000, discounting the $3,000. Also, in the secondary market, a discount is the amount less than face value that a buyer of a mortgage pays in order to be induced to take out the loan. The discount here is calculated on the basis of risk, market rates, interest rate of the note, and other factors. (See **Points.**)

Dual Agent: An agent who expresses loyalty to both buyers and sellers and agrees to work with both. Only a few agents can successfully play this role.

Due-on-Encumbrance Clause: A little noted and seldom-enforced clause in recent mortgages that allows the lender to foreclose if the borrower gets additional financing. For example, if you secure a second mortgage, the lender of the first mortgage may have grounds for foreclosing. The reasoning here is that if you reduce your equity level by taking out additional financing, the lender may be placed in a less secure position.

Due-on-Sale Clause: A clause in a mortgage specifying that the entire unpaid balance becomes due and payable on sale of the property. (See **Acceleration Clause.**)

Escrow Company: An independent third party (stakeholder) that handles funds, carries out the instructions of the lender, buyer, and seller in a transaction, and deals with all the documents. In most states, companies are licensed to handle escrows. In some parts of the country, particularly the Northeast, the function of the escrow company may be handled by an attorney.

FHA Loan: A mortgage insured by the Federal Housing Administration. In most cases, the FHA advances no money, but instead insures the loan to a lender such as a bank. There is a fee to the borrower, usually paid up front, for this insurance.

Fixed Rate Mortgage: A mortgage whose interest rate does not fluctuate for the life of the loan.

Fixer-Upper: A home that does not show well and is in bad shape. Often the property is euphemistically referred to in listings as a "TLC" (needs tender loving care) or "handyman's special."

Foreclosure: A legal proceeding in which the lender takes possession and title to a property, usually after the borrower fails to make timely payments on a mortgage.

FSBO: For sale by owner.

Garbage Fees: Extra (and often unnecessary) charges tacked on when a buyer obtains a mortgage.

Graduated-Payment Mortgage: A mortgage whose payments vary over the life of the loan. They start out low, then slowly rise until, usually after a few years, they reach a plateau where they remain for the balance of the term. Such a mortgage is particularly useful when you want low initial payments. It is primarily used by first-time buyers, often in combination with a fixed rate or adjustable rate mortgage.

Growing Equity Mortgage: A rarely used mortgage whose payments increase according to a set schedule. The purpose is to pay additional money into principal and thus pay off the loan earlier and save interest charges.

HOA: Home Owners Association, found mainly in condos but also in some single-family areas. It represents home owners and establishes and maintains neighborhood architectural and other standards. You usually must get permission from the HOA to make significant external changes to your property.

Index: A measurement of an established interest rate used to determine the periodic adjustments for adjustable rate mortgages. There are a wide variety of indexes, including the Treasury bill rates and the cost of funds to lenders.

Inspection: A physical survey of the property to determine if there are any problems or defects.

Jumbo: A mortgage for more than the maximum amount of a **Conforming Loan**.

Lien: A claim for money against real estate. For example, if you had work done on your property and refused to pay the workperson, he or she might file a "mechanic's lien" against your property. If you didn't pay taxes, the taxing agency might file a "tax lien." These liens "cloud" the title and usually prevent you from selling the property or refinancing it until they are cleared by paying off the debt.

Loan-to-Value Ratio (LTV): The percentage of the appraised value of a property that a lender will loan. For example, if your property appraises at $100,000 and the lender is willing to loan $80,000, the loan-to-value ratio is 80 percent.

Lock In: To tie up the interest rate for a mortgage in advance of actually getting it. For example, a buyer might "lock in" your mortgage at 7.5 percent so that if rates subsequently rose, he or she would still get that rate.

Low-Ball: To make a very low initial offer to purchase.

MAI: Member, American Institute of Real Estate Appraisers. An appraiser with this designation has passed rigorous training.

Margin: An amount, calculated in points, that a lender adds to an index to determine how much interest you will pay during a period for an adjustable rate mortgage. For example, the index may be at 7 percent and the margin, agreed upon at the time you obtain the mortgage, may be 2.7 points. The interest rate for that period, therefore, is 9.7 percent. (See also **Index, Points.**)

Median Sales Price: The midpoint of the price of homes—as many properties have sold above this price as have sold below it.

MLS: Multiple Listing Service—used by **Realtors** ® as a listings exchange. As much as 90 percent of all homes listed in the country are found on the MLS.

Mortgage: A loan arrangement between a borrower, or "mortgagor," and a lender, or "mortgagee." If you don't make your payments on a mortgage, the lender can foreclose, or take ownership of the property, only by going to court. This court action can take a great deal of time, often 6 months or more. Further, even after the lender has taken back the property, you may have an "equity of redemption" that allows you to redeem the property for years afterward, by paying back the mortgage and the lender's costs. The length of time it takes to foreclose, the costs involved, and the equity of redemption make a mortgage much less desirable to lenders than a **Trust Deed.**

Mortgage Banker: A lender that specializes in offering mortgages but none of the other services normally provided by a bank.

Mortgage Broker: A company that specializes in providing "retail" mortgages to consumers. It usually represents many different lenders.

Motivated Seller: A seller who has a strong desire to sell. For example, the seller may have been transferred and must move quickly.

Multiple Counteroffers: Comeback offers extended by the seller to several buyers simultaneously.

Multiple Offers: Offers submitted simultaneously from several buyers for the same property.

Negative Amortization: A condition arising when the payment on an adjustable rate mortgage is not sufficiently large to cover the interest charged. The excess interest is then added to the principal, so that the amount borrowed actually increases. The amount that the principal can increase is usually limited to 125 percent of the original mortgage value. Any mortgage that includes payment **Caps** has the potential to be negatively amortized.

Origination Fee: An expense in obtaining a mortgage. Originally, it was a charge that lenders made for preparing and submitting a mortgage. The fee applied only to FHA and VA loans, which had to be submitted to the government for approval. With an FHA loan, the maximum origination fee was 1 percent.

Personal Property: Any property that does not go with the land. Such property includes automobiles, clothing, and most furniture. Some items such as appliances and floor and wall coverings are disputable. (See also **Real Property.**)

PITI: Principal, interest, taxes, and insurance. These are the major components that go into determining the monthly payment on a mortgage. (Other items include home owner's dues and utilities.)

Points: A point is 1 percent of a mortgage amount, payable on obtaining the loan. For example, if your mortgage is $100,000 and you are required to pay $2^{1}/2$ points to get it, the charge to you is $2,500. Some points may be tax deductible. Check with your accountant. A "basis point" is 1/100 of a point. For example. if you are charged $1/2$ point (0.5 percent of the mortgage), the lender may refer to it as 50 basis points.

Preapproval: Formal approval for a mortgage from a lender. You have to submit a standard application and have a credit check run. Also, the lender may require proof of income, employment, and money on deposit (to be used for the down payment and closing costs).

Prepayment Penalty: A charge made by the lender to the borrower for paying off a mortgage early. In times past (more than 25 years ago) nearly all mortgages carried prepayment penalties. However, those mortgages were also assumable by others. Today virtually no fixed rate mortgages (other than FHA or VA mortgages) are truly assumable and, hence, few carry a prepayment penalty clause. (See **Assumption.**)

Private Mortgage Insurance (PMI): Insurance that protects the lender in the event that the borrower defaults on a mortgage. It is written by an independent third-party insurance company and typically covers only the first 20 percent of the lender's potential loss. PMI is normally required on any mortgage that exceeds an 80 percent **loan-to-value ratio.**

Purchase Money Mortgage: A mortgage obtained as part of the purchase price of a home (usually from the seller), as opposed to a mortgage obtained through refinancing. In some states, no deficiency judgment can be obtained against the borrower of a purchase money mortgage. (That is, if there is a foreclosure and the property brings less than the amount borrowed, the borrower cannot be held liable for the shortfall.)

Real Property: Real estate. This includes the land and anything appurtenant to it, including the house. Certain tests have been devised to determine whether an item is real property (goes with the land). For example, if curtains or drapes have been attached in such a way that they cannot be removed without damaging the home, they may be spoken of as real property. On the other hand, if they can easily be removed without damaging the home, they may be personal property. The purchase agreement should specify whether doubtful items are real or personal to avoid confusion later on.

Realtor®: A broker who is a member of the National Association of Realtors. Agents who are not members may not use the Realtor designation.

REO: Real estate owned—a term that refers to property taken back through foreclosure and held for sale by a lender.

RESPA: Real Estate Settlement Procedures Act. Legislation requiring lenders to provide borrowers with specified information on the cost of securing financing. Basically it means that before you proceed far along the path of getting the mortgage, the lender has to provide you with an estimate of costs. Then, before you sign the documents binding you to the mortgage, the lender has to provide you with a breakdown of the actual costs.

Second Mortgage: An inferior mortgage usually placed on the property after a first mortgage. In the event of foreclosure, the second mortgage is paid off only if and when the first mortgage had been fully paid. Many lenders will not offer second mortgages.

Short sale: Property sale in which a lender agrees to accept less than the mortgage amount in order to facilitate the sale and avoid a foreclosure.

SREA: Society of Real Estate Appraisers—a professional association to which qualified appraisers can belong.

Subject To: A phrase often used to indicate that a buyer is not assuming the mortgage liability of a seller. For example, if the seller has an assumable loan and you (the buyer) "assume" the loan, you are taking over liability for payment. On the other hand, if you purchase "subject to" the mortgage, you do not assume liability for payment.

Subordination Clause: A clause in a mortgage document that keeps the mortgage subordinate to an existing mortgage.

Title: Legal evidence that you actually have the right of ownership of **Real Property.** It is given in the form of a deed (there are many different types of deeds) that specifies the kind of title you have (joint, common, or other).

Title Insurance Policy: An insurance policy that covers the title to a home. It may list the owner or the lender as beneficiary. The policy is issued by a title insurance company and specifies that if for any covered reason your title proves defective, the company will correct the title or compensate you up to a specified amount, usually the amount of the purchase price or the mortgage.

Trust Deed: A three-party lending arrangement that includes a borrower, or "trustor"; an independent third-party stakeholder, or "trustee" (usually a title insurance company); and a lender, or "beneficiary" so-called because the lender stands to benefit if the trustee turns the deed over in case the borrower fails to make payments.

The advantage of the trust deed over the mortgage is that foreclosure can be accomplished without court action or deficiency judgment against the borrower. In other words, if the property is worth less than the loan, the lender can't come back to the borrower after the sale for the difference. (See also **Purchase Money Mortgage.**)

Upgrade: Any extra that a buyer may obtain when purchasing a new home—for example, a better-quality carpet or a wall mirror in the bedroom.

Upside Down: Owing more on a property than its market value.

VA Loan: A mortgage guaranteed by the Veterans Administration. The VA actually guarantees only a small percentage of the loan amount, but since it guarantees the first monies loaned, lenders are willing to accept the arrangement. In a VA loan the government advances no money; rather, the mortgage is made by a private lender such as a bank.

Wraparound Financing: A blend of two mortgages, often used by sellers to get a higher interest rate or facilitate a sale. For example, instead of giving a buyer a simple **Second Mortgage,** the seller may combine the balance due on an existing mortgage (usually an existing first) with an additional loan. Thus the wrap includes both the second and the first mortgages. The borrower makes payments to the seller, who then keeps part of the payment and in turn pays off the existing mortgage.

Index

Locators in **bold** indicate 'terms to know'

About the Author

Robert Irwin, one of America's leading experts in all areas of real estate, is the author of more than 40 books, His *Tips and Traps* series for McGraw-Hill has sold over a million copies. A broker and property investor as well as advisor to consumers and agents, he has helped buyers and sellers solve their real estate problems for more than 20 years. He lives in Westlake Village, California. For more real estate tips and traps, go to www.robertirwin.com.